# FREE TO BE YOU

by

## DR. FRED ANTONELLI

MORFX Press

Smyrna, Delaware

Published by Morfx Press,
a division of Missional Press
149 Golden Plover Drive
Smyrna, DE 19977
www.missional-press.com

Printed in the United States of America

ISBN: 10: 0-9798053-3-3
ISBN: 13: 978-0-9798053-3-2

Cover design by Sam Raynor, www.iamandsam.com.

Library of Congress Control Number: 2008929768

# Table of Contents

# Dedication

**To those who have struggled:**
In the quest to be liberated of wounding self-definitions that have
hampered your ability to see the greater YOU that God has
purposed for this earth, may this book provide some
encouragement and insight toward your journey on being
FREE TO BE YOU.

# Acknowledgements

To my wife Debbie for your endless dedication to our counseling practice. What you have been gifted to do has been absolutely invaluable and your help with this book has been so greatly appreciated...I love you!

To Gary for your tireless editing work...you're fantastic at what you've been gifted to do. Thank you so much for taking my Jib-Jab and making it legible.

To Sam, your unbelievable talents in art work and design are truly a blessing from God! Never stop expressing the art that He's birthed in you!

And to Dave, thank you for your vision in helping people dream dreams! You're making a difference in the lives of many by virtue of the person that you have been called to be.

# About the Author

Dr. Fred Antonelli is founder and director of Life Counseling Center with offices in Easton and Salisbury, Maryland as well as Dover, Delaware. He is a Certified Marriage and Family Temperament Therapist specializing in Crisis Marriage and Pastoral Counseling.

Dr. Antonelli has served as a Senior Pastor for twenty-three years. He also was host for nine years of the popular nationally syndicated Christian teen and young adult radio show, Rock Alive, heard over both the CBN Radio Network and the Salem Radio Network. Aside from being a licensed psychotherapist, he is also a seminar speaker, conference speaker, and business coach as well as a consultant to churches through leadership training, conflict resolution, and church restructuring.

Fred holds a BA in Theology, an MA in Clinical Counseling and a Ph.D. in Clinical Psychology.

Fred and his wife Debbie have three grown children and live in Easton, on the Eastern Shore of Maryland.

# Foreword

"Who am I?" has always been a difficult question for us to answer. With all of the peer pressures and cultural expectations of our day and age, perhaps this has become the hardest question to answer. In our attempts to answer the question, we often pick some role we play that is important to us and use it to define our answer. Most men will say that "I am what I do"—especially my work. Most women will say the same kind of thing, such as "I am Zachary's mom." But pressed beyond what we do, and we often don't have an answer. Someone has said that we are not "human-doers" but we are "human-beings." But if the questioner says, "I want to go beyond what you do, to who you are," we are at a loss for words.

Dr. Antonelli has tackled this question of "who am I" and helps take us step-by-step on a journey of self-definition—what kind of "being" are we? Weaving together his pastoral experience with his clinical experience, he has creatively provided tools we can use in practical ways to break away from what he calls the "messages and signals" of our family-of-origin, and from the cultural pressures that have often trapped us into an understanding of ourselves that isn't really who we are.

Beginning with the ability to dream again—to envision what stirs deep within us, Fred goes on to combine your dream with God's dream for your life. Then he lays out practical ways you can nourish yourself so that you can persevere on the path God wants to lead you on so as to enjoy your life. In these pages you will find ways to redefine yourself that are biblically based, rather than culturally based. And when you dig in to this book, you will find out how to answer that "who am I" question. Enjoy the journey!

David Stoop, Ph.D.
Author and Psychologist

# Preface

The issue of the destiny of our lives is very serious, because it concerns the most important question for man: the purpose for which he was placed on earth. If man takes the correct position on this subject, if he discovers his actual purpose and destiny, he can then take the correct position on life's most important questions. Questions such as his relationship with God as well as with people around him, his purpose, his profession, his opinion of himself, his marriage, his parenting abilities, his quest to succeed in life, and his longing for a promising future. However, if he does not take the right position nor come to the right conclusion when addressing these crucial questions, then he will be setting himself up for a fall when it comes to reaching his life goals. In actuality, what purpose can goals possibly have if human life has been robbed of its true meaning?

The question of what we can do to give purpose and meaning to our lives has been debated for thousands of years by philosophers, religious leaders, and everyday common men and women. Yet today we seem further from the answer than ever before. Despite our great material wealth and high standard of living, people are grasping for something that money cannot buy and materialism can not satisfy. The famous journalist, media critic, and philosopher Walter Lippmann said, "Our life, though it is full of things, is empty of the kind of purpose and effort that gives to life its flavor and meaning."

The title, FREE TO BE YOU means just that, free to be the gifted and talented person that you were originally designed to be by virtue of your Creator God. Free to walk away from the destructive "coded messages" that have been implanted into your psyche perhaps since childhood. Free to be able to nourish your mind, soul, spirit, and body in a way that will literally catapult you into knowing what it feels like to live a vibrantly successful and emotionally secure life! And free to be able to celebrate the great expression of amazement that you really are - personally, relationally, occupationally, and spiritually!

FREE TO BE YOU will take you on a journey that will lead to a place that is filled with hope and healing for a more confident today and a brighter tomorrow. This book comes out of working with teenagers, individuals, married couples, and business professionals for over thirty three years as a former senior pastor as well as a licensed psychotherapist. In the final analysis, all of us are really the same. We are all born into family systems that, in some way, have affected us positively or negatively, more often on the negative end. As a result, those affects tend to play out in the way that we treat others as well as the way we view ourselves. Consequently, we end up defining

4

who we are by virtue of how other people, in particular our parents, treated and labeled us. "You'll never amount to anything.".... "Your brother/sister is smarter than you." ... "You're stupid." ... "You just can't do it right."... "That isn't good enough, do it better." ... "How long before you screw it up." ... "Second place isn't good enough, why didn't you make First?!" These and other messages from your childhood have great power over how you view yourself in virtually every area of your life.

This book is dedicated to every soul who was robbed of their true God-given identity and has wandered on their own personal trail of tears, trusting and praying that they would somehow receive help for today and hope for tomorrow. My prayer is, that in the pages of this book, perhaps in some small way, that help and hope can be realized!

Dr. Fred Antonelli, 2008

## Chapter One

# A Different View of You

Have you ever taken the time to really evaluate yourself? Have you ever asked the question, "What do I really think of me and how do I view myself?" So often we're sizing up other people and looking at either the positive points or defects in their lives, those things that encourage us or bug us about others. You know what I mean; the person behind you in the supermarket line who runs his cart into the back of your ankle! Or how about the guy in the car behind you who blasts his horn because you let a pedestrian finish crossing, or how you have to inform five different sales people in the same store that you're "just browsing!" As the ditty goes, "It's the little things that bother us and put us on the rack, you can sit upon a mountain but you can't sit on a tack."

But how about you? How do you think others would view the way that you act in public or the way that you would respond when finding yourself in an irritating moment? How do you perceive YOU? Yes, we all have idiosyncrasies; we all fall short to some degree by the way that we would like to act in any trying or stressful situation. But the question is, do you see the blemishes and weakness in your life more than you see the qualities and strengths? Is it difficult for you to receive a compliment or feel that you actually have something to offer that is valid and worthwhile? And if you do feel that you have something of worth to offer, do you share it confidently, or do you hesitate, feeling like perhaps it wasn't really that important anyway?

Self-image or self-worth is both a conscious and subconscious way of seeing yourself. It is the emotional and personal critiquing you take on that helps form your self-worth. Actually, the foundation of our self-image is developed in early childhood by our parents. How they talked to you, the words they chose, whether they were critical or encouraging, the body language they showed and the patience they gave or didn't give contributed greatly to just why you feel the way you do about you.

Having a positive self-image can be challenging, especially if you've been affected by any of life's hardships, such as a disability, poor health, childhood traumas, a moral indiscretion, financial difficulties, or other related problems. The mere fact that these pressing issues find there way into so many of our lives, should cause us to want to find out how we can constructively address them without having them define us. But unfortunately, they do tend to define so many people; consequently, they become imprisoned in their own self-perception.

Franklin D. Roosevelt ( 32nd President of the United States) said, "*Men are not prisoners of fate, but only prisoners of their own minds.*"[1] FDR could say this through personal experience, because he was a man, who at age 39, was stricken with polio, a fearsome and incurable disease that paralyzed his legs for the rest of his life. What do you do with a problem like that? How do you face the challenges of each day with such a debilitating disease? How do you view yourself as well as how you feel others view you? Are your todays paralyzed? Are your tomorrows crushed? For those of us who have been fortunate enough to not have had such a sickness, we probably really don't know how we would approach each day. It's difficult to relate with this type of hardship unless you have actually experienced it!

FDR's attitude toward his illness was inspirational when it came to his outlook for the future: "*The only limit to our realization of tomorrow will be our doubts of today. Let us move forward with strong and active faith.*"[2] He could have taken all of his hopes and dreams and suppressed them within the confines of four walls and a wheelchair, but he didn't; he took a different view of himself despite his physical limitations! With faith, determination, and resolve, FDR went on to become one of the greatest presidents that this country has ever seen! But what separated him from others that battled similar conditions? Or even others that face physical, emotional, or physiological

9

challenges? I believe he viewed himself differently than the way people viewed him. Others saw him as a cripple; he viewed himself as just having to be more creative when it came to maneuvering. Others saw him as limited in what he could do and accomplish, he viewed himself as limitless by virtue of the gifting and talents bestowed upon him by his Creator. So much of "what we do" effects "who we are!" The reverse can be said as well. Who **I am** can greatly effect what **I do**. The perspective for accomplishments is found in how you view yourself. When a person is secure in who they are, there is nothing that can interfere with their success, emotionally, spiritually, relationally, or occupationally. I'll address this in more detail later in the book.

## The You View Test

People view themselves in different ways. Some are like the Little Train That Could. Even though the odds are against them, their confidence level soars to the occasion under pressure and they're determined to accomplish the task no matter how difficult the challenge. Their motto is, "I can do it, I have what it takes, nothing can stop me if I put my mind to it." Still others, no matter how often they're encouraged by friends or family, have convinced themselves that they just won't reach their goal regardless of how hard they try. Their motto seems to be, "why try, in the end, I'm going to fail anyway!"

Take a look at the questions below and see if any of them tend to describe your view of YOU.

- Do you avoid mirrors or any reflections of yourself?
- Do you wish you could re-shape your body or looks?
- Do you worry about gaining weight?
- Do you feel that your worth is determined by your appearance?
- Do you find yourself wishing that you were someone else?
- Do you feel that others have more to offer and say than you do?
- Do you see the glass half-empty more than half-full?
- Do you find it hard to take a compliment?
- Do you always apologize for things?
- Do you constantly criticize yourself?
- Do you bend over backwards to please others?
- Do you feel that most people are smarter and more talented than you?
- Do you feel that because of personal failures, you're unworthy of success?

- Do you feel there are vices in your life that are hindering a healthy self-image?

If several of the above describe you—and most people can relate to at least a few—then it's time that you consider working on a different view of you! Maxwell Maltz said, "*Self-image is the key to human personality and human behavior.*"[3] As long as you continue to allow your unhealthy view of you to dominate your self-concept, you will be defined by who you "feel" you are rather than who you were originally designed to be.

## Where It Began

A lot of our personal imagery foundation was laid at childhood. One well-respected and proven tool for family development in this area is a theory called Systemic Therapy. Arguably, the greatest pioneer in this field was famed Family Systems expert, Dr. Murray Bowen (1913-1990) a professor of psychiatry at Georgetown University and founder of the Georgetown Family Center. Systemic Therapy is the conscious attempt and method to study, understand, and cure disorders within, what is known as, the "Nuclear Family" (father, mother, brothers and sisters). These disorders usually can be passed down from one generation to the next and have the tendency to effect the way we think and act out as adults. The clinical term used here is called Object Relations. The premise is that there are three fundamental "effects" that can exist between you and the others in your family - *attachment, frustration,* and *rejection.* These effects are universally emotional and can act as major building blocks toward infecting our personality for good or for bad!

Looking at the chart below, in which box do you relate in terms of childhood experiences?

| Healthy View of YOU | Poor View of YOU |
| --- | --- |
| Childhood experiences that lead to a healthy view of YOU include:<br>• being praised and given affirmation<br>• being listened to and feeling important<br>• being spoken to respectfully and kindly<br>• being shown affection and feeling deeply loved<br>• experiencing success in sports or school | Childhood experiences that lead to a poor view of YOU include-<br>• being harshly criticized or made to feel stupid<br>• being yelled at, or beaten/abused<br>• being ignored, ridiculed or made fun of<br>• being expected to be "perfect" all the time<br>• experiencing failures in sports or school |

As you can clearly see, there is a dramatic difference in the box on the left from the box on the right. A healthy or poor view of ourselves, based on our childhood experiences, goes a long way in how we perceive and view the person that we are, or, the person that we've become. There is good news and bad news here. Let's look at the bad news first. If we continue to live in our "wounded frame of mind", that is the wounding and pain that we've experienced from our childhood, then there is a tendency to act that out through our adulthood. Example: If you were screamed at and criticized as a child by either mom or dad, there is the likelihood that you could do the same thing to your children and even your spouse! Conversely, if your parents used a calm and non-aggressive tone when correcting you as well as avoided criticism when speaking to you, there is the likelihood that you could act the same way toward your children and spouse.

There's a lot of truth to the old phrase, "I act this way because that's the way my father was!" Well, that may indeed be the case, but to know "the cause" of just why you act out the way you do, has the potential to be personally liberating, not only for you, but for those who are closest to you in life. Personal enlightenment isn't just about searching for something; it's about punching holes in the darkness that has negatively affected us throughout our lives. It's a journey of wanting to become aware of the unaware and then acquire the tools so as to be free to be the YOU that you were meant to be! Benjamin Franklin once said: "*There are three things extremely hard: steel, a diamond, and to know one's self.*"[4] Old Ben was right, to know the person that you really are requires an honest introspective evaluation of yourself, not the easiest thing for any of us! To have a clear awareness and understanding of that amazing creation called YOU, that is your strengths, weaknesses, shortcomings, destructive patterns, talents, gifting, etc, is to then possess the keys that open the doors to a successful life! To not consider this is to view ourselves "one dimensionally". That means that I would look at myself and say one of three things: (1) "In the final analysis I have little to offer and much to work on." (2) "I have a lot to work on, so I better get busy." or (3) "I am who I am, so it's others that need to work on themselves to accept me." If we're not open to other dimensional views of ourselves, other meaningful possibilities, then the only thing left is our capacity for self-deception. We then deceive ourselves in believing that there is only "one string" on our life's guitar that we're destine to plunk throughout our journey, when in actuality there are five more that have the potential of making beautiful sounding cords! So again, our personal imagery foundation laid at childhood is without question a contributing factor in both the way that we act out as adults and how we perceive ourselves.

If we could only catch a glimpse of the powerful statement the cartoon character Pogo meant when he gazed into the mirror and said, "*We have met the enemy and he is us!*" It's true! We tend to be our own worse enemy when it comes to defining who we are. Our objectivity toward us can be, and often is, blurred on either side by how we view ourselves, both negatively as well as positively. To consider a different view, an objective view, an honest and open view of the YOU that was "*fearfully and wonderfully made*" (Psalms 139:14) is to discover an endless wealth of exciting and dynamic possibilities that await YOU!

# Chapter Two

# You and Your Identity

Rollo May said, "*Joy, rather than happiness, is the goal of life, for joy is the emotion which accompanies our fulfilling our natures as human beings. It is based on the experience of one's* <u>*identity*</u> *as a being of worth and dignity.*"[1] I believe one of the greatest tragedies that befall most all of us, is our never ending appetite for the "pursuit of happiness." Let me try to put this into perspective. Remember seeing bumper stickers proclaiming every conceivable source for happiness? One said, "Happiness is being married." Another countered, "Happiness is being single." One cynical sticker read, "Happiness is impossible!"

For most people happiness is possible, but it's also fickle, shallow, and fleeting. As the word itself implies, happiness is associated with happenings, happenstance, feelings, luck, and fortune. If circumstances are favorable, you are happy; if not, you're unhappy. Happiness is a feeling. It comes and goes as much as our circumstances around us change. Joy on the other hand is different. Joy is steady and constant. The person experiencing joy vs. just happiness has laid an emotional foundation that supports both good times and bad times as well as times of elation and sadness equally. Joy does not ultimately

17

respond or react to our outward circumstances; instead, it reflects the power of balance and steadiness that exists on the inside of us. Happiness sees and responds to the temporal, joy sees and responds to the eternal.

Unless we are willing to look beyond just the "happy feelings," we will then ultimately end up being prisoners of whatever "feeling" is defining us in that moment. Whether that is a rush of excitement as a result of winning the lottery or feeling depressed because you didn't get that job promotion. Consequently, to know what "defines you" and where that comes from, that is, the messages and signals that have adversely affected you, is to be able to move from darkness into light when it comes to your identity! Of course all of us can, and often do, have those feelings. But when your identity is based on defining yourself as an unhappy, fearful, intimidated, depressed, low achieving, anxious, little-to-offer, angry, critical person, then there has been "something" that has interfered with the identity you were originally meant to have! In other words, who are you really? And what are the God-given talents, gifting, and abilities that you were originally meant to express in life? Who is the real YOU outside of the above mentioned negative defining words? Let's take a journey to see if we can discover that amazing YOU and the true identity that you were meant to experience!

## Signals and Messages

I've read several definitions for identity, but after teaching and counseling people for over thirty years, here is Fred's version: "*The unique spiritual, behavioral & temperamental definition of who we are designed by God to be.*" Unless you see yourself as the talented and gifted person that you were meant to be through your "unique" expression, then you're destined to be defined by how you "feel" about you rather than who you were originally designed to be!

To effectively address the SIGNALS & MESSAGES that have been burned into our psyche since childhood is to be free of the emotional weights and chains that prevent us from being successful in every area of our lives! This is the principle of symptom/cause. Symptom: low self esteem, anger, and sensitivity to constructive criticism. Cause: was never told that you could do anything right, a father who acted out in anger toward you and berated you on almost every front! It's the messages and signals from your past that are trying to convince you that this is who you are and how you act out when "triggered" in your present. Think of it this way, your mind is the garage door. There is a key pad with numbers that is attached to the outside of your garage. When you press the hand remote, the door responds to the sequence of numbers that have been programmed into the unit. Consequently, the door automatically goes up or down by virtue of the "signals" or "messages" sent to it. It's the same thing that happens when you are triggered by someone or something that reminds you of a negative or traumatizing experience from your past. When someone presses that remote in you, the messages and signals cause you to respond or react in a way that may not at all be positive or constructive for you or the other person! If you multiply these episodes throughout the course of your life, then there is the potential for you to "feel" that this has become part of your identity, the thing you do, your emotional DNA! In actuality, it isn't at all, although the messages and signals are doing their best to try to convince you that it is! Then, as a result of the "frequent transmitting" of these signals and messages from our past, what happens is, we receive them, then we believe them! In other words, you actually end up believing that this is the person that you really are! That somehow this is the way that you were designed to interact with others. When this stage happens, the identity process would appear to be complete; you become convinced that this is the YOU that you are to be throughout the course of your life. I call this the Lock and Load theory. Messages and signals locked into your psyche from childhood...loaded as potential "self definition" ready to be shot out to do damage in your adulthood. Aren't you glad that FDR didn't give in then give up to the definition of his illness? If he had, perhaps we might be speaking German or Japanese now! If this theory connects with you, then consequently, I would encourage you to not give in and give up to what you "feel" has been your definition or identity so far!

## De-Code / Re-Code

So then how do you combat these negative signals and messages that tend to define you?  Abraham Lincoln, speaking of the great challenges of the Civil War said, "*The dogmas of the quiet past, are inadequate to the stormy present. The occasion is piled high with difficulty, and we must rise with the occasion.*"[2] In order to effectively address the [seemingly] quiet and distant past as well as the "stormy present" in your life, you need to think about stepping up to the plate and "*rising [to] the occasion!*"[3] I'd like for you to consider something that I call De-Code / Re-Code! That would mean first "decoding" or, decrypting the scrambled signals/messages that have been causing emotional, relational, and even spiritual damage throughout the years.  Those signals/messages have been transmitted and lodged in your psyche since childhood. Each time life's hand remote triggers you by someone or something that reminds you of the childhood message, you then will respond either positively or negatively! These wounding childhood messages, if not dealt with, become instrumental in defining the way you act, think, reason, and respond to any given interaction, in particular when you find yourself engaged in stressful situations. There are times that people may realize that they have inconsistencies in their lives that cause disruption. But, too often they don't know "why" these inconsistencies don't get better. So it becomes very important for you to first want to decode or decrypt these messages so as to clearly understand what they are, where they came from and how they have emotionally affected you throughout the years. Let's take a look at a few negative signals and messages that tend to originate from childhood that need to be De-coded.

## <u>DE-CODE</u> (Your Negative Signals/Messages)

- **The Need To Feel Approved** (Tell Me I Matter)
- **Feelings of Worthlessness** (Not Feeling Important Or Valued)
- **Inferiority** (I Have Nothing To Offer)
- **I'll Never Achieve My Goals** (Defeatism)
- **Feelings of Inadequacy** (I Fall Short Of Success )
- **Feeling Like You're Damaged Goods** (PTSD)
- **I Can't Stack Up** (I Could Never Do It Good Enough)

- **I'm Stupid** (Messages Implanted From Childhood)
- **I'm Not Worthy Of Being Loved** (I Don't Like Who I Am)
- **I'm Unforgivable** (My Sin Is Too Great)

These messages have defined more incredibly gifted human beings than you could possibly imagine! Take for instance Post Traumatic Stress Disorder (PTSD), a common anxiety disorder that develops after exposure to a terrifying event or ordeal in which grave physical harm occurred or was threatened. If you've experienced this in life, then there is a huge chance that your trauma has greatly contributed to how you view yourself. For instance, if you were the victim of sexual abused as a child, it tends to scar virtually all facets of your life leaving you with little or no self-esteem as a result. Some of the social challenges stemming from such an abuse are alcoholism, drug addiction, prostitution, and promiscuity. Eating or sleeping disorders, migraines, night traumas, and back or stomach pains are just a few of the physical symptoms that a victim may suffer.

Food, sex, alcohol, and/or drugs numb painful memories of the abuse and alter reality temporarily. Then, if a victim as an adult, encounters someone who reminds them of their childhood abuser, they will become fearful, anxious, feel unsafe, and do all

she would start but seldom finish a household task, as a result, the house was always unkempt and disorganized. Consequently, Bill felt the only way to motivate Lynn into completing a project around the house was to yell at her and point out her inconsistencies and shortcomings! As we probed deeper into Bill's family history, I found out that Bill's dad was an alcoholic and a harsh man who often screamed at his mother as well as him and his two brothers. He was also very critical and even demeaning, particularly when he was drinking! There were also times when his father would resort to physical abuse by pulling his mother's hair and beating Bill and his brothers with a belt when things weren't completed to his expectation around the house. You may be able to guess what the signals and messages were that Bill received from his childhood. With Bill, in order to get someone to do what you want them to do, you had to scream at them and intimidate and demean them into submission! So even though Bill wasn't an alcoholic or physically abusive, he was still emotionally and verbally abusive. Remember the quote, "I act this way because that's the way my father was?" Well, as you can see, it panned out in the life of Bill as well! So therefore the messages were, "I must yell, scream, and demean to get my way, therefore, I'm a yelling, screaming and demeaning person, that's who I am!" No Bill, that's "what you DO" but that's not "who you ARE!"

Have you caught the common thread that is woven through each of these three examples? I believe Rocky Balboa expressed it best in Rocky 3 when he said to his wife, Adrian, while struggling to train for a fight on the Philadelphia ocean shoreline, *"Nothing is real if you don't believe in who you are, I don't believe in myself no more!"*[4] That's it! When you fail to believe in who you are, your chances to succeed dwindle greatly. It doesn't matter where you are in life, what your status is, or what you've acquired in getting there. When you don't believe in the amazing you, that beautiful and influential expression that God has created, then nothing about you can be really appreciated by you, because you've become falsely defined by the coded messages! Like the strings attached to a marionette, you're pulled this way and that, regardless of the way you'd like to go you always end up going in the direction that the puppeteer chooses! You know, the neat thing about Pinocchio was that he didn't want to settle for being something that wasn't authentic! A wooden puppet walking around mimicking a real boy wasn't his idea of the kind of life he wanted for himself! People may have seen him as just a hunk of painted wood and stings, but he saw himself as a "real boy!" Something legitimate and authentic! Don't allow yourself to be defined by the strings that have pulled you thus far in life. Refuse to allow the coded signals and messages to define you any longer! If they do, they will rob you of your true God-given emotional DNA and identity, that is the incredible talented and gifted person that you were meant to be and meant to express!

So then, how do you begin to understand and appreciate your true identity? How do you get rid of those negative coded messages and signals that have held you back in so many areas of life? The answer would be to RE-Code them! To put in the intended code, that is the proper signals/messages as per how your Creator sees you and has uniquely designed you from the foundation of the world. Let me say here that this process may very well require the help of a trained professional psychotherapist that specializes in Family Therapy. But if you should decide to journey here, the possibilities become endless when it comes to you discovering the greatness of the person that you are! Let's look at your original coded messages as per how your Heavenly Father sees you and has always seen you.

## RE-CODE  (Your True IDENTITY)

### Forgiven
*(though I am sinful and fall short)*

Hannah Arendt once said, "*Forgiveness is the key to action and freedom.*"[5] The very word itself denotes being pardoned or liberated from either a wrong suffered or given.

On a spiritual level, God is a forgiving God, and His very nature is to extend Himself in both love as well as forgiveness to all who ask Him. God's deep desire is to reconcile the fallen heart of mankind and unite it back to Himself. "*The LORD is long-suffering, and of great mercy, forgiving iniquity and transgression.*" Numbers 14:18 (KJV)

Aside from its spiritual benefits, Forgiveness has the ability to release the mind and the heart from all past hurts, failures, resentments, guilt, shame, humiliation, anger, and loss. The emotional and physical benefits of forgiveness below are worth noting:

- Decreased anxiety
- Decreased depression and grief
- Decreased anger and irritation
- Decreased vulnerability to substance use
- Decreased chronic pain and cardiovascular problems
- Eliminates blame, bitterness and hostility linked to unforgiveness
- Increases joyful experiences as well as faith and hope

Paul Boese put it best when he said, "*Forgiveness does not change the past, but it does enlarge the future.*"[6] Forgiveness doesn't do away with the fact that you were either wronged or

29

As difficult as it may seem at times, you are not the only one who feels like the only one! There are many souls that feel great emotional or psychological pain and travel in life wondering if healing and relief will ever visit them. Even in the midst of your sorrow and pain, God is there to help provide an anchor when life's stormy weather tries to sink your hopes and dreams! One of the Hebrew names in the Old Testament for God is Jehovah Rapha. The name translated means, "*Lord God Our Healer.*" I need to point out here that having a faith doesn't automatically make you free from experiencing pain in life anymore than living in Orange County, California automatically makes you an orange grower. But to know that there is One that walks beside you to heal and console as well as eventually bring life into what would appear to be a lifeless situation, is to experience part of your identity! His committed availability (even when it appears at times that He is unapprehendable) is designed to be your strength in the midst of questions, uncertainty, disappointments, and even trauma. In the words of Dr. Martin Luther King Jr., "*We must accept finite disappointment, but never lose infinite hope.*"⁹ Your refuge and healing lies in the hands of Him who is lovingly there for you in the backdrop of life's struggles. Part of who you are is your ability to hope! Hope transcends all limits and crushes all barriers that set themselves out to define you! To accept the emotional healing that is available for you, is to dare to reach into the darkness and touch the One who can stabilize you until the night is gone and the morning breaks again!

## Loved
(*though I feel unlovely*)

Since the beginning of time, the number one greatest longing in all human beings is the need to both be loved and express love. Aside from the biological/sexual component, love can be defined as a deep, tender, yearning feeling of affection and concern toward another person. Without this one paramount human ingredient, mankind would cease to genuinely and honestly connect in visceral relationships. One of the greatest and simplest quotes I've ever heard on love was from Mother Teresa, "*The hunger for love is much more difficult to remove than the hunger for bread.*"[10] Everyone hungers for love, but not everyone feels lovable! But even though a person may not feel that they are worthy of being loved, still, deep inside of them they desperately cry out for it...the need can't be removed because it's been woven into the emotional fiber of every human being.

Your negative childhood messages, shortcomings, mistakes, and personal failures in life may have left you feeling not only unlovable to others, but also unwilling to peer into and consider the greatness of the person of who you were created to be. The knowledge of knowing that you are deeply and unconditionally loved by your Creator, regardless of your history, is without question the key in liberating you to experience and celebrate your purposed identity!

## Strong
*(as a result of first acknowledging my weaknesses)*

American author, poet, and philosopher Ralph Waldo Emerson once said, *"Our strength grows out of our weakness."*[11] The Apostle Paul put it slightly different when he said in 2 Corinthians 12:10, *"...for when I am weak, then am I strong."* (NAS) The unmistakable message here is, unless you own the weaknesses and character flaws in your life that are weighing you down and consequently denying you emotional, relational, occupational, and spiritual success, then strength of personal character will evade you! Your strengths for success can only be brought to the forefront as you first acknowledge the weaknesses that have held you back in life. This is without question one of your top challenges, because you were not originally programmed to honestly self-evaluate your personal shortcomings. By nature all of us are much quicker to point out the speck in the other person's eye rather than the log sticking out of our own eye!

In Aesop's Fable, "The Dog and the Oyster," we see a great analogy for wisely considering your weaknesses:

*A DOG, used to eating eggs, saw an Oyster and,*
*opening his mouth to its widest extent, swallowed it*
*down with the utmost relish, supposing it to be an egg.*
*Soon afterwards suffering great pain in his stomach, he*
*said, "I deserve all this torment, for my folly in thinking*
*that everything round must be an egg.* [12]

The moral of the story being, they who act without sufficient thought, will often fall into unsuspected danger. To acknowledge the fact that you can act out in ways that place you at a disadvantage in life and shrink your possibilities for achievement, can be a very wise choice when positioning yourself for success in life! To reach inside of you and be willing to observe what others witness when they view you, and then take that as constructive criticism for helping mold you into a better person, is to experience in part the strength of who you really are. If not, everything round has to look like an egg and therefore, not being aware of the pain that's on its way, you keep doing the same thing and keep getting the same results!

# Significant
(*as a person even though my past may try to rob me of this truth*)

Often when I ask people in a counseling session if they feel significant and secure as a person, I tend to get some pretty interesting answers.  Probably the most popular response is, "I'm not sure, I think I am, but then again, because I'm hesitating, that probably means I'm not!"  If it's any consolation, most people don't support a strong sense of personal significance when describing themselves.  The word significant means a sense of importance, having meaning and recognizing quality.   With most people, seeing themselves with these attributes is a tall glass of water to drink and difficult to accept.

When you factor in the messages and signals from your childhood as well as any personal failures, mistakes or shortcomings from your adult life, you can begin to see just why you may not feel very significant!  But when discovering the person that you were meant to be, that is your specific and originally customized identity, rather than the person that you see, things then can look quite different!  Do you recall the old saying, "seeing is believing?"  Well it proves true when positioning yourself for success in life.  If there is no clear view when driving, flying, or operating equipment, then accidents happen!

Sometimes those accidents can be devastating!  Your past may be robbing you from being able to view the significant person that you are.  But daring to believe these Re-Coded messages has the potential of liberating you to a place where you have never been in your life!   A place of security, stability, productivity, confidence, and renewed faith!  It really doesn't get much better than that!

## Talented/Gifted
*(though I find this hard to see in me)*

Psalms 139:14 says that you are *"fearfully and wonderfully made"* by God.  Aside from His amazing ability to create such a specimen as a human being, He has also "pre-loaded" it with fantastic talents and gifts!  For example, to witness the untold beauty and inspirational magnificence of the paintings on the ceiling of the Sistine Chapel, is to be amazed at the unspeakable talent and artistic genius of its creator, Michelangelo.   To view the art is to see the man and his God given abilities.  Mother Teresa gave hope and healing to tens of thousands as a humanitarian and advocate for the poor and helpless in India.  Her deep love for God and endless devotion of ministry to the oppressed people of India won her the respect and admiration of multiple leaders from around the world.   While practicing law in Illinois, Abraham Lincoln met an old woman in dire poverty who was the widow of a Revolutionary soldier.  She was charged $200 for getting her $400 pension. Lincoln sued the pension agent and won the case for the old woman. He didn't charge her for his services and, in fact, paid her hotel bill and gave her money to buy a ticket home![13]

You may be thinking, "That's really inspirational Fred, but I'm no Michelangelo, Mother Teresa, or Abraham Lincoln!" You're right, you're not! But you are YOU! The problem with reading or hearing about inspiring stories, is that we somehow feel that they only pertain to "other people." We seldom, if ever, think that "we" can actually be "them!" Gifting and talents are not just given to certain people in life; they're given to "everyone!" Jan Paderewski, the famed Polish pianist and composer, was asked by a fellow pianist if he could be ready to play a recital on short notice. The famous musician replied, "*I am always ready, I have practiced eight hours daily for 40 years.*" The other pianist said, "*I wish I had been born with such determination.*" Paderewski replied, "*We are all born with it, I just used mine.*"[14] To tap into and use your hidden gifts and talents is to discover a treasure of abilities and qualities that were meant for you to beautifully express in life! Everyone is born with talents and gifts. Perhaps messages from your past or mistakes in your present have caused you to have a lower opinion of any attributes that you may possess. You need to know that negative life experiences does not nullify God given inspiration! Whether it's through the arts, acts of humanitarian kindness, expressions of sensitivity and love, abilities in business, hospitality, a heart of servitude, or any other of the endless God given expressions, know that you too are blessed with divine gifting!

# Unique
*(though I feel there's nothing extraordinary about me)*

American modern dance pioneer and choreographer Martha Graham said when speaking of the individual qualities of a person, *"There is a vitality, a life force, an energy, a quickening, that is translated through you into action, and because there is only one of you in all time, this expression is unique."*[15]  Having been raised as a strong Presbyterian, she was keenly aware of the great attributes that God had given both men and women.

In Act 17:28, the New Testament tells us that, *"He [God] gives us the power to live, to move, and to be who we are."* (CEV).  To be who YOU are...that is to be the uniquely designed and highly gifted person that was specifically and deliberately expressed by your Creator!  To be who YOU are is to lay hold of the unparalleled individual characteristics that were methodically placed in your DNA at conception.  Each aspect and expression of your being is amazingly extraordinary in nature.  The way you talk, react, express your emotions, respond to a need, word what you feel, think, dream, love, smile, walk, express your talents and gifts, etc.  All of these aspects of you and more make up the unique and unusual pattern that allows you to "be who [you] are!"  Of course, as a result of negative life experiences or traumatizing childhood imagery, the thought of you being unique probably is the furthest thing from your mind!  Hermann Hesse put it this way, "*Every man is more than just himself: he also represents the unique, the very special and always significant and remarkable point at which the world's phenomena intersect, only once in this way, and never again.*"[16]

Being unique is who you are, it's part of your true identity and individual make up and expression.  You or no one like you will ever grace this planet again.  Even your children, though they share some of the same genetics as you, will never be able to display your unique qualities, temperament and gifting...you're really one of a kind and worth exploring!

## Approved and Accepted
(*though I've been told I fall short*)

Just why is the need for approval and acceptance from our parents, family member, peers, and colleagues so very important to us?  The need for that slap on the back, that encouraging word or smile from our boss, parents, or friends is really important to each one of us because it tells you that what you have done is good, acceptable, and noteworthy.  The need for both approval and acceptance is a powerful need within each one of us. Without realizing it, the need for approval can control a lot of what we do and greatly influences how we interact with others.

Actually, the need for approval comes from a low sense of self, a feeling of being unworthy. One of the problems in defining your own worth is that you may have been programmed to see yourself through the eyes of your parents, teachers, siblings, and peers. When you were growing up, if you were judged, criticized, rejected, or ridiculed, you may have then begun to believe other people's view of you. You may have bought into their assessment of you not realizing the fogginess of the glasses that they were actually looking through. In other words, it is their own issues that cause them to be so critical toward others. So in all fairness, you can't really define your own worth and lovability from your wounded self - your coded programmed mind. You need to define yourself through the eyes of your true identity, not the eyes of judgmental, wounded, and angry others.

Bill Hybels, senior pastor of Willow Creek Community Church in South Barrington, Illinois said, "*God wants to father all of us until we're dead sure of His approval, His guiding power and His promise of heaven.*"[17] You see, you were designed to ultimately receive and emotionally benefit from God's approval of you, not the approval of others! Though receiving approval from others can be beneficial and helpful, in particular from your spouse or close loved ones, you need to know that ultimately, your source of approval is Father connected not people projected! If you get this in reverse, you must then be defined by what others say about you and how they view and critique you. You're not free then to be you, but rather subject to how others dissect you from their unhealthy perspective of life. Someone offering you sensitive constructive criticism is one thing, but harsh insensitive comments are unacceptable in any case! Ecclesiastes 9:7 says, "*Go then, eat your bread in happiness and drink your wine with a cheerful heart; for God has already approved your works.*" (NAS). No one is expected to feel God's approval if they are doing something that is wrong or harmful to themselves or others. But God has, through His Son, purchased for all of humanity the ability to be free of unworthy and insignificant feelings. He "has already approved your works," and there is nothing that you can possibly do to have Him approve you more than He already does! To journey into a deeper relationship with your Heavenly Father is to experience a more secure sense of self as well as a clearer understanding of that gifted you! In the end, I believe St. Augustine said it best, "*Grant, Lord, that I may know myself that I may know thee.*"[18]  God is the true source as well as the illuminator of your amazing and spectacular identity!

## Chapter Three

# Your Amazing Temperament

In order to effectively appreciate and comprehend the true person that you are, you need to understand your inborn genetic temperament. Temperament, simply defined, is a person's inborn manner of thinking, behaving, and emotionally reacting. It is a person's genetic disposition as well as their mental and physical characteristics resulting from dominance of the four humors: Sanguine, Melancholy, Choleric, and Phlegmatic.

Temperament research is an important aspect of the study of human psychology; it emphasizes the importance of a person's individuality. Historically, in 450 B.C. Hippocrates, who is known as the founder of medicine and was regarded as the greatest physician of his time, described four dispositions he called temperaments. A Choleric temperament with an ease of emotional arousal, sensitivity, and control; a Phlegmatic temperament with cool detachment and a sympathetic nature; a Melancholy temperament with a critical, downcast, and self contained nature; and a Sanguine temperament full of impulsivity, excitability, quick reactivity, and social ability. In 1984, a fifth temperament type was discovered by Drs. Richard and Phyllis Arno, called "Supine."[1] The Supine temperament type is characterized by a tendency toward indirect behaviors and an inability to initiate. They are of a gentle nature and often find it difficult to say no to people. These individuals characteristically find themselves as being people pleasers. This fifth temperament type is beginning to be used more and more by those in the counseling and mental health profession.

## Why Is Temperament Relevant to You?

The whole human community can be regarded as a system, holistic in nature, seeking survival and relationship. Throughout the ages, those observing human behavior have repeatedly identified four major patterns of behavior. These behavior patterns have been recorded for at least twenty-five centuries. Understanding the five temperaments (including the Supine temperament) gives profound insights into your deep motivations, core psychological needs, core values, talents, and communication patterns.

Most twentieth-century psychologists abandoned holistic observation of human behavior for a microscopic examination of parts, fragments, traits, and so on. To them, all human beings were basically alike, and individual differences were due to chance or conditioning. Two German psychologists, Ernst Kretschmer and Eduard Spränger, were among the few to continue to view individuals holistically in terms of patterns. Inspired by their work, a modern psychologist, David Keirsey, noted common themes in the various observations and the consistent tendency of human behavior to sort itself into four patterns. Being similar to Melancholy but in other ways different, Drs. Richard and Phyllis Arno went on to develop the Supine as a fifth type that has been very helpful in identifying new characteristic traits that have greatly benefited individual and family therapy. Another noted temperament specialist was famed Russian psychologist Ivan Pavlov. Dr. Pavlov placed people into the same four types as Hippocrates. His findings have greatly influenced temperament theory to this day. So in summarizing, even though it is a theory, your temperament basically explains why you do the things you do!

## Temperament, You and the God Factor

Everyone has been hardwired by God with a specific temperament or temperament blend. Your temperament is an X-ray of your emotional make-up as well as a peek into your genealogy. You're something like Mom, Dad, Aunt Bertha and Great-great Grandpop Jones! You have certain genealogical traits and patterns stemming from both sides of your gene pool.

In Isaiah, 51:1-2, it appears that God is saying that we should look back at our ancestors to catch a more accurate view of ourselves.

*The LORD says, "Listen to me, those of you who try to*
*live right and follow the LORD. Look at the rock from*
*which you were cut; look at the stone quarry from*
*which you were dug. Look at Abraham, [your father],*
*and Sarah, who gave birth...[consider your ancestors]."*
*(NCV)*

You've probably heard the old expression, "He's a chip
off the old block!" Well, looking to the "rock from which you
were cut," and "the stone quarry from which you where dug" has
a tendency to fit here. In other words, if you want to live a
productive, successful, and meaningful life with the least amount
of shortcomings and relational baggage, it behooves you to look at
your genealogical patterns, both the positive and negative aspects
of your inborn temperament types! Each one of these
temperaments can also have what is known as blends. This
simply means that it is possible for any of the five temperament
types to blend into another, example, Choleric/Phlegmatic.
The Psalmist David tells us in Psalm 139, that God "*created*
*[your] inmost being.*" Paul D. Meier, MD, Frank B. Minirth,
MD, and Frank Wichern, Ph.D., in their book, Introduction to
Psychology and Counseling, Christian Perspectives and
Applications, agree that character and behavior defects are
correctable. "Through Divine inspiration, although he knew
nothing about DNA and RNA, David knew that before we were

born, God designed us!"   They went on to say, "While your body was being differentiated within your mothers womb, each "inward part" was designed exactly as God intended, including both your strengths and weaknesses.  We have the responsibility of living up to our potential, correcting any correctable defects".[2]  God did His part by creating us, now we need to do our part by taking responsibility for the weaknesses that can wreak havoc in our lives!  Taking a healthy look at your temperament can make the difference between successful self- evaluation and blinding failure!

## Your Temperament Breakdown

The exciting part of your temperament is that it's "individualized!"  Again, even though you share certain genetic traits from your genealogy; still, you're an amazingly specific and deliberate work of your Creator!   Let's take a look at some of the Pros and Cons of each of the temperament types.

## Sanguine

| Strengths | Weaknesses |
|---|---|
| • Optimistic / Lively <br> • Social / Talkative <br> • Fun-filled / Warm <br> • People person <br> • Spontaneous | • Tends to interrupt <br> • Emotional (cry...yell) <br> • Temper tantrums <br> • Great starter / slow finisher <br> • Lustful |

47

## Melancholy

| Strengths | Weaknesses |
| --- | --- |
| • Task oriented<br>• Sets high standards<br>• Gifted (arts...design...mechanics etc)<br>• Financially responsible<br>• Deep thinker / Analytical | • Critical<br>• Moody<br>• Negative<br>• Shows little affection<br>• Introvert |

## Choleric

| Strengths | Weaknesses |
| --- | --- |
| • Personable<br>• High energy<br>• Inspiring<br>• Born Leader<br>• Dogged determination | • Strong willed<br>• Can lack compassion<br>• Hot tempered / Impatient<br>• Controlling<br>• Bossy |

## Phlegmatic

| Strengths | Weaknesses |
| --- | --- |
| • Sensitive<br>• Imaginative<br>• Kind hearted<br>• Feeling based / Intuitive<br>• Considerate | • Vulnerable<br>• Fearful<br>• Sharp with words<br>• Stubborn<br>• Unforgiving |

## *Supine*

| Strengths | Weaknesses |
|---|---|
| • Optimistic | • Non-assertive |
| • Servants heart | • Difficulty saying No |
| • Accommodating | • A people pleaser |
| • Compassionate | • Defensive |
| • Team player | • Easily placed under guilt |

## The Three Parts of Temperament

Everyone's temperament is made up of three specific areas. It's worth noting that there can exist what is known as blends in each of these below categories. That would mean it's possible that you could be a blend of two temperaments in any category, for example, Supine/Phlegmatic. These three categories are:

**Inclusion** - communication /socialization

**Control** - dominance / the will

**Affection** - the emotions

In the *Inclusion* part of you, there is a need to communicate (connect) with others. You want to understand as well as be understood by both close and peripheral relationships. The need and desire to communicate differs from person to person. Some people have a great need to talk, interact, socialize and be part of anything that seems to be going on around them. A Sanguine would fit the bill here. With them, any conversation is a good conversation. They love to talk, socialize and go places...it really doesn't matter where they go, they just like being active! Others have much less of a need to communicate or talk. Take the Melancholy for instance, to be engaged in long conversations with one or more people can appear painful to them. Matter of fact, their motto seems to be, "the less talking the better!" They're very practical and really only want to enter into conversation when there is need to do so. In other words, "If there's a reason for us to communicate, then let's talk. When the reason for talking is over, so am I!" As far as the Melancholy socializing...this to can appear to be painful as well! Often, they feel much more comfortable by themselves or with someone else that they have become comfortable with. They don't seek out socialization and much prefer the least amount of people to people interaction as possible. The only time that they don't appear to have a problem socializing is when there is a "purpose" for it. There has to be a need, a purpose, a reason for socializing, then it's ok, at least for a while.

With the *Control* part of you, there is a need in everyone to make decisions for themselves and take on responsibilities. There is a certain dominance and act of the will to either be independent or dependent. For instance, if you are Choleric in the control area of your temperament, then you prefer to have a great deal of control over other people's lives and behaviors. Although, when it comes to others assuming control over you, this is not something that you take easily! By nature a Choleric is a controlling personality. They also are good leaders, inspire others, and are determined to carry things through to completion. On the other hand, if you are Supine in the control area of your temperament, you strain in making decisions or taking on responsibility independently. Often you need a trusted person who will help you make decisions and take on responsibilities. Supines are people pleasers by nature and would rather disappoint themselves than disappoint others.

Looking at your *Affection,* there is a need in each of us to both give as well as receive emotional connectedness. Everybody wants to be loved and shown affection, even if it appears that some people struggle with it. Let's say that you are Phlegmatic in the affection part of your temperament, then you will tend to be a calm, easy going person who is not plagued with the emotional outbursts, exaggerated feelings, anger, bitterness, or unforgiveness as that of other temperaments. The Phlegmatic appears to be equally as comfortable being an extrovert as an introvert. They seem equally comfortable showing or not showing love and affection. If you're this type of temperament, then you do not get very involved with deep personal relationships and don't expend a lot of energy to keep the relationships going. Phlegmatics are calm, easy going peacemakers who are rather flexible when it comes to giving and receiving affection. If you are Sanguine, then you have a much greater need to show love and affection and a great need to receive it! Contrasting, let's look at the Melancholy, when it comes to affection. Because of their tendency of having low self-esteem and introversion, they find it very challenging to show the tender emotions that they have. The law of reciprocity (the more love you give, the more love you receive) doesn't fall into play here. Out of all of the temperaments, the Melancholy has the least need for receiving and showing affection. Consequently, overt displays of tender emotions or showing the "warm and fuzzies" are very rare with the Melancholy temperament.

## Your Temperament and Relationship Success

All relationships face similar challenges when it comes to interacting. Actually, it's how you respond that makes or breaks the union. Relationships can be between two people or several people. There must be something to relate around–whether the commonality is values, life-theme, career, faith, family, shared history, or philosophy of life. Each of us has our own way of communicating. For instance, the language of affection that two people express so easily on some days can fall apart on other days and neither can figure out why! Often two people can believe they are clearly communicating their needs and values, when in fact little gets through, because each is coming from different core assumptions. They interpret remarks and body language differently and look for a completely different set of messages from the other person. Even self-explanatory words like passion, trust, intimacy, commitment, and respect can be communicated differently depending on the person's interpretation. Each temperament has its own language and meaning. The key is to know your temperament well enough so as to take ownership of the challenging parts that can cause friction and conflict within a relationship. This could be with your spouse, a significant other, a friend, a co-worker or business associate. To know and understand the language of your temperament is not only hugely beneficial when it comes to maintaining a stable relationship, but it also allows you the insight and freedom to be that incredible you!

The thing you can absolutely count on in a relationship is that you will act according to your temperament core needs, values, life-themes, and beliefs that paint who you are and how you were genetically programmed. When there are difficulties, you do not always need to "fix" the other person or distance yourself if you can't. You can consider giving the other person some space to be who he or she was purposed to be by virtue of God's specific design for them. And you do not have to make it your goal to change the other person or even yourself for that matter! To succeed in any relationship as well as in life, only consider changing the negative parts of your temperament that can prove detrimental or unhealthy. To put this into practice is to experience what it feels like to be that unique YOU as well as allowing others the same celebration!

## Temperament and Your Emotions

When it comes to your emotions, every human being, no

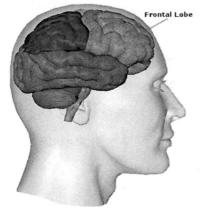

Frontal Lobe

matter what their temperament, operates from the same 3 ½ pound computer..."the brain!"

The frontal lobe of the brain is considered our emotional control center and home to our personality or temperament traits. The frontal lobe is involved in motor function, problem solving, spontaneity, memory, language, initiation, judgment, impulse control, and social and sexual behavior. Your inborn DNA has a lot to do with the way you both process and express in each one of these categories. Let's take a peek into the "emotional control center" of the temperament types and team them together in relationship.

### Melancholy meets Sanguine

The Melancholy temperament is normally a laid back person that really is not happy because deep down they don't like who they are. They have a tendency to set very high standards for themselves as well as with others. The Sanguine on the other hand is not laid back at all and projects a very up beat and vibrant attitude. They actually don't like to set standards at all and don't hold others to setting standards either. Let's put a few frontal lobe principles into play here.

### Problem Solving Factor

When it comes to solving problems or conflicts that requires the Melancholy to engage emotionally, normally he will procrastinate, not feeling comfortable overtly expressing himself. He needs time to consider, ponder and think through what to say and even then, if he had his preference, he'd like to table the whole issue and just let it work itself out. Conversely, the Sanguine sees problem solving as an opportunity to express like an artist paints a picture, using exciting and colorful words and a lot of them! They need no time to ponder their thoughts; they're ready in a split second and would rather not table any issue, because as far as they're concerned, it's an opportunity to express their feelings. Their frontal lobe is kicking in like a bored and stroked 327 Chevy engine! Solving problems requires "talking" and "communicating" and they are strong at both!

### Supine meets Choleric

The Supine temperament is a sensitive and compassionate person who is normally very accommodating and caring. Although because of their low self-esteem, they can often feel like a victim and exhibit a weak will to stand up and share what they "really think" concerning an issue. They have a difficult time saying "no" and then end up feeling used in the process! The Choleric responds from quite a different perspective. This person is very practical and decisive, they know exactly what they want and the way they want it. They can be very charming and appear very much in control. Unlike the Supine, they have no problem at all expressing what they think or feel concerning any given issue. They can be opinionated, domineering, impatient and even bossy at times. Where the Supine doesn't necessarily make the best leader, the Choleric does. These two temperament types have a tendency to be drawn to one another. The Supine likes the "takeover" confident style of the Choleric and the

Choleric likes the non-aggressive accommodating style of the Supine.

### The Impulse Control Factor

When it comes to impulse control, the frontal lobe kicks in very differently with these two temperaments. Because the Supine is a laid-back person by nature, they will have the tendency to be more cautious and even seem to procrastinate when making a decision. Remember, Supine is similar to Melancholy so they will be less impulsive and more reserved when approaching in relationships, be that intimate or business relationships. Being quick, confident, and ready to respond in conversation is not something that defines a Supine. They are not impulsive people but rather can appear friendly, but reserved and cautious at the same time. The only impulse they may have is in not being able to say no! They will impulsively say yes to people even though they may not at all want to do the thing they're saying yes to! They are typically placed under guilt because of their low-self esteem, this is one of the reasons Cholerics are drawn to them, they can be persuaded to do something easily.

The Choleric on the other hand can be very impulsive and make decisions at the drop of a hat. It is very easy for them to make decisions for themselves and it's very easy for them to

make decisions for others as well!  This is the initial drawl for the
Supine because they like other people making the decisions.
Although, in time if not being considered or made to feel
important, the Supine will begin to resent the Choleric because
they become tired of being taken advantage of.  The Choleric has
a lot of high energy and dogged determination, so they can
respond impulsively without doing a lot of "considering" before
reacting!  You may be thinking, "How can such polar opposites
be drawn to one another?"  Here's where the saying, "opposites
attract" comes into play.  Each has something that is attractive to
the other.  Believe it or not, if both work on the negative parts of
their own temperament, they actually have the potential of making
a very good relationship combination.

### Phlegmatic meets Melancholy

This combo is really interesting because both can come
from a "stubborn" position!  Phlegmatics are easy going, well
balanced, sympathetic people.  They're not the quickest people
when it comes to completing a task, although they usually get the
job done.  They often don't use their ideas and talents because it
requires too much energy and participation to put these ideas into
action.  They appear lazy at times when it comes to accomplishing

things and will try to inspire others to do what they're not willing to do.

### Social and Sexual Behavior

The Phlegmatic temperament, like the Melancholy, is task oriented. They are also very precise people when it comes to making sure things are accurate. If they become hurt or offended, they can be "wordy" and express with a "bite!" Like a Melancholy, they can have a dry sense of humor, only the Phlegmatic can have "quicker comeback" remarks. For example, if you were to tell a Phlegmatic that he/she should trade cars, they would most likely come back with something like, "Yeah, I'll run right out and buy a new car and send you the coupon book!" Or, "Wouldn't that be convenient? I buy the new car and you get to drive it!" Their stubborn nature and dry sense of humor can make for an interesting social relationship when teamed with a Melancholy because the Melancholy type can be stubborn, critical, and dry humored as well. If neither work on the negative parts of their temperament, be they intimately involved or simple in a business relationship, you're talking about a "cool and distant" atmosphere! So as you can see, the emotional control center can respond quite differently from temperament to temperament. Another note of interest is that every person can also be affected emotionally by virtue of their family systems and learned behavior. Temperament has very much to do with the way we think, behave and emotionally react, but it isn't the only factor. It's important to remember this when looking at the full dimension of YOU!

In terms of sexual involvement, the Phlegmatic can appear to be cool and complacent. They seldom overtly give affection and are not really upset if they do not receive affection. When they do show affection, it is shown slowly and with little energy. Although interestingly, if they are shown affection or are given sexual advances from their spouse, they will respond in an affectionate/sexual way. They are so well rounded emotionally, that whether shown or not shown affection, they appear ok with it, they can respond either way without getting upset. When you mix this with the Melancholy who has a low affection rate as well as a low sex drive, this becomes an emotionally doable relationship...very little "spice" but doable!

In summary, since temperament is God-given and inborn, it's important to realize that—no matter how you try—you cannot change who you are and how you've been made. Although in making that statement, you should also know that it is very possible to address the "negative parts" of your temperament that cause discontent and irritation within a relationship. When a person undergoes changes in their behavior because they have learned how to overcome the temperament weaknesses, these changes then have a high likelihood of being permanent. This is a very good thing when looking at you and relational/emotional connections.

## Chapter Four

# You and Self-Talk

What we tell ourselves about ourselves—our self talk—will either create success or defeat in our lives. Our success depends so much on the messages we constantly send ourselves. We can be our best friend or we can be our own worst enemy. Each of us has the capacity of affirming ourselves or of sabotaging our own belief in who we have been designed to be by our Creator. And the difference between constructive self-criticism and destructive criticism can be so small yet the difference in effect can be huge!

A personal example of destructive self talk:

I remember an experience in the gym when I had just finished my workout on both the treadmill and weights. I realized I was telling myself that what I had just done wasn't much of an exercise, that I should have pushed harder - increased the time of the workout - burned more calories - increased the poundage on my weights - done more abs work - did more than what I had done! I was telling myself that an hour an a half workout on 9 machines just wasn't enough! I was telling myself that what I had done was not good enough. Wow! An hour and a half workout four times a week for a 57 year old man in a day when any form of exercise is a push for anybody just didn't seem to be enough!

And then to end it with a dose of self criticism for not doing something different or better...self sabotage at its best - or worst! Then I realized, I do that a lot with myself. I minimize my accomplishments and think of them as less than what I should or could be doing. Do you ever do that?

Destructive self-talk is the result of negative messages. The messages that say you should do more, that what you've done isn't that great; that compared to others you don't measure up, has the long term effect of creating in your mind a feeling of not being good enough...not being worthy! Again, this kind of information is coming from the messages and signals that we talked about in Chapter Two. Take a good look at your own self-talk and see if it builds you up or tears you down. Do you find that you minimize most things that you do? Do you feel that you should have done something else or what you did just wasn't good enough? Do you feel that most people can do things better than you? If so, then you need to work on getting that kind of non-constructive self-talk out of your mind and heart. The good news is that kind of destructive self-talk just isn't true. The better news is that you have the capacity and ability within you to change it. And the best news is you can start to change it today! It's not easy, many people have been doing it for so many years that it seems a natural thing to do. But never forget this: "*In order to get what you have never gotten, YOU must be willing to do what you have never done!*"

This is without question the first and foremost ingredient for success in life and a key in being free to be YOU! If you're not willing to consider this, then all that's left is the definition for insanity, "Doing the same thing every day expecting a different result!"! Now you're talking about living in the preverbal "gerbil wheel!"

## How You Begin

First, become aware that you're doing it. And then work hard to replace those messages that have buried themselves into your psyche with the purpose of defining you as less than you were created to be. Choose to begin to work at seeing yourself the way you have been specifically designed and expressed by God to be! Be determined to break the habits of self-condemnation and personal inabilities! Dr. Carl Gustav Jung, the famed Swiss psychiatrist said, "*We cannot change anything until we accept it. Condemnation does not liberate, it oppresses.*"[1] Truer words have never been spoken! Self-condemnation that limits the spectacular greatness of the person that God has created you to be is the poison apple that is meant to destroy your identity and prevent any lasting form of success in your life!

Second, learn to become proactive in identifying your self-criticism. Ask yourself what you can do better as well as how you can make it better. If whatever you're doing is sincere, thought out and honest, then it's quality! Any other message is a lie that says "It just isn't good enough!" Take what you are learning about you and apply it to your present and future rather than mourning over your past. It's a subtle shift, but what you are doing is shifting from the negative self-criticism that has been defining you, to a more positive, successful, and healthy self-image. Looking at what you are truly and honestly attempting to accomplish and not liking it, is throwing you back into the abyss of self-doubt and defeatism! Again, that "does not liberate, it oppresses." What a rotten place to live! You can definitely do better!

Third, build into your mind, heart and soul a Mantra! Though the term may originate from Hinduism and Buddhism, still the purpose and meaning is just as relevant to Christians or any other faith as well. A mantra is primarily used as a spiritual conduit that instills a one-pointed concentration in the devotee. It's a sacred phrase, scripture, or word that is used as part of meditation and prayer to aid in developing a more spiritual awareness and power within you. A mantra has the power and persuasion to help calm and steady your mind and heart whenever you're anxious, depressed, feel defeated, or need emotional strength in general. There are other positive techniques such as counting to ten, taking deep breaths, or repeating a positive affirmation to yourself. These are all good and helpful, but your mantra is something that comes from deep within your soul, something that is so meaningful and personal, that it becomes soaked with faith, hope, and encouragement! Actually, this life skill is thousands of years old. Saint Francis of Assisi, for example, repeated *"My God and my all."*[2] Mother Teresa's mantra was, *"Lead me from the unreal to the real, lead me from darkness to light, lead me from death to immortality."*[3] To come up with your own personal intimate mantra has the potential of instilling great fortitude, strength, faith, and encouragement in you during challenging times. It gives you a more healthy perspective on life and creates within you a type of emotional shield that helps you withstand the destructive forces that are out to hinder and cloud your potential.

### How can a Mantra Help You?

- It calms you down, regardless of what you may be facing or going through.
- It helps you from reacting too quickly or saying something or responding in a way that you may regret later.
- It helps you feel more balanced and gives you a better perspective on what you're facing.
- It reduces rising anger, fear, panic, and anxiety.
- It encourages you and increases your faith to trust and believe that you can accomplish your goal.

- It puts distance between you and your challenge. Once you repeat your mantra, you'll find yourself in a much safer place to choose your next move.

When you establish your mantra and begin to use it, you'll find that it has the potential of working fast! You'll probably feel the benefit of it the next time you face a difficulty or challenge. In Philippians 4:8 it says, *"Finally, brethren, whatsoever things are true, whatsoever things are honorable, whatsoever things are just, whatsoever things are pure, whatsoever things are lovely, whatsoever things are of good report; if there be any virtue, and if there be any praise, think on these things."* Clearly the Apostle Paul is instructing that your mind should "think (or dwell) on these things," a type of mantra. The old phrase, "you are what you eat" certainly falls into play here. What you dwell on, take in, meditate on, and concentrate on will tend to have a powerful effect on your frame of mind as well as the emotional, spiritual, and relational development of your life. Paul went on to say in verse nine that if you *"practice what you have learned and model your way of living on it...the God of peace (of untroubled, undisturbed well-being) will be with you."* It's that "untroubled, undisturbed well-being" that you want for yourself! A mantra helps you to get there through the trying irritations of life and provides just the needed edge that will push you over the top to a safer more settled and productive place.

## You and Self-Talk Questions

One very creative and useful thing that you can do is come up with messages that you can send yourself that are positive and proactive. The only way to get rid of a bad habit is to replace it with a good one. Below are some questions to ask yourself to get those positive and productive messages flowing:

- What makes you so special? Remind yourself that you are unique by God's design and there is not a single person on the face of the earth that can express themselves exactly like you.

- What are your special and unique contributions (gifting and talents)? How can you best use them?

- How can you more effectively use your personal experiences, education, skills, interests and talents today?

- What can you apply to your life today that you learned from yesterday?

- In what ways can you use your mantra in helping build your self-esteem and confidence?

- How can you use your faith today in helping you to succeed in life? (The Bible is a great source of awe-inspiring quotes and confidence boosting ideas. Your faith is the most powerful tool you possess in making yourself stronger!)

- In what ways can you be easier on yourself? Learn how to forgive yourself and move on.
- In what ways can you help others? You will feel happier and more satisfied as you "give out" of the kindness and compassion that God has placed in you. You will also experience a deeper respect for yourself as well.

## Who is the Me You See?

In looking at a Mantra or a "tag on" to your mantra, consider this phrase: "*The me I see is the me I will be, who is the me I see?*" How you visualize, critique, and feel about yourself has so very much to do with not only your identity, but also how you position yourself for life success. If you have fallen into the habit of negatively defining yourself, then you have dammed up the reservoir of possibilities in your life!

Bruce Lee, the famed martial arts instructor and movie actor once said, "*All fixed set patterns are incapable of adaptability or pliability. The truth is outside of all fixed patterns.*"[4] If you have been defining you by self-defeating and negative fixed patterns, then you have been damming up your reservoir of life possibilities as well as limiting yourself to adapt and be pliable for future options.

On Halloween morning in 2003, 13 year old Bethany Hamilton was on her surfboard in clear waters off the coast of

Kauai's North Shore in Hawaii when a shark, later estimated by authorities to be between 12 and 15 feet long, bit off her left arm just below her shoulder and disappeared. Despite the trauma of the incident, Hamilton was determined to return to surfing. Just ten weeks after the incident, she returned to her board and went surfing again. She adopted a custom-made board that was longer and slightly thicker which made it easier to paddle. She observed that she had to kick a lot harder to make up for the loss of her left arm. After teaching herself to surf with one arm, she has again begun surfing competitively.

Bethany Hamilton's deep faith in Christ mixed with a supportive family and a very strong determination to not be victimized by defeat, went on to receive the 2004 ESPY Award for Best Comeback Athlete of the Year. She was also presented with a special courage award at the 2004 Teen Choice Awards. Her book, *Soul Surfer: A True Story of Faith, Family, and Fighting to Get Back on the Board,* has inspired thousands of people to forge ahead regardless of their challenges!

Bethany could have very easily seen herself as a crippled traumatized young girl unable to any longer compete in the sport that she loved so much. But instead she refused to see herself in that way. Instead she viewed herself in the way "she would be," not the way she was left to be. Having now only one arm was a challenge Bethany took on. She was determined to not dam up the reservoir of her possibilities in life but rather seize the day and refuse to give into negative self-definition. Bethany refused to take on a fixed pattern to her injury. Consequently, she become pliable to a new way of life and adapted to changes that eventually led her to excel in her sport! She would be nothing less than what her Creator had designed and defined her to be...a success in life's journey![5]

Who is the me you see? Perhaps your experience in life isn't as dramatic as Bethany Hamilton's. But with any of us, life has a way of biting down on our hopes, dreams, and aspirations without ever being aware of its full intentions. But with faith, determination, and positive reinforcement, your world can be a very different place to live in!

Self-talk then has the valued potential to reach into the inner you that so desperately needs rescuing and bring out in you the richness of the person that you really are! This isn't some nebulous mind over matter technique, but rather a "tapping into" something that already exists in you, something that lives in the core of your very being and hand placed there by your Creator! Self-talk helps stir the life juices that too often find themselves dormant in the lives of wounded souls. Abraham Lincoln said, *"If you are resolutely determined to make something of yourself, the thing is more than half done already."*[6] Just stepping up to the plate and saying, "With God's help I CAN do this" is already accomplishing half the task!   Self-talk is saying and uniting with the thing that already dwells within you, all you're doing is bringing it out and allowing it to live!

## Chapter Five

# You and the Power of Ownership

This is something that definitely doesn't come natural to any of us! Being able to take personal *ownership* (responsibility) of your words, actions, conduct, intentions, and lifestyle is a tall glass of water for anyone to drink. But nonetheless, when acted on, it has the rich potential of being personally, relationally, emotionally, spiritually, and occupationally rewarding! Ownership without a doubt is a key in relational and occupational success. It also goes a long way in helping you to identify just "who you are" in terms of successful communication skills and qualities.

Personal Ownership is being "fully accountable" for results that matter to you in life. The more important something is to you, the more you have to be willing to assume responsibility. It is about controlling life events rather than being controlled by the events. Personal ownership requires a transformation in thinking. It takes a revaluating or even a reinventing of the way you normally deal with conversations, interpersonal relationships, and decision making. In order to take ownership and hold yourself accountable, the topic of your attitude and behavior needs to be addressed.

Life success depends 10% on what comes your way, and 90% on how you react to it. Meaning, you have 100% control over how you choose to react in any given situation that life throws at you. No one can upset you, disappoint you, ruin your day, or control your emotions unless you give them permission to do so. No one can "force you" to react in an undesirable or unhealthy way, your reaction originates from within!

## You and the Blame game

Blame is the oldest game known to man! It was invented by Adam and Eve who, after eating of the forbidden fruit, told God, "*The woman whom You gave to be with me, she gave me of the tree, and I ate*" (Genesis 3:12). In other words, *it's Eve's fault* that I did this, and, indirectly, God's fault! Not a whole lot has changed since that day in the garden. You can ask just about anyone when something falls apart or didn't work out and they will point to someone or something else. In my experience, it is very rare for people to stand up and take personal responsibility for their part in a particular issue, especially a "relational" issue!

The bad news about taking ownership is that you can't blame someone else. It always comes down to your integrity and longing to see the issue brought to an honest conclusion. There is always something else you could have said or done to make it seem like it was the other person's fault, not yours! But the good news is that once you accept ownership, you now are in the driver's seat to be able to change the result. Why? Because your behavior as a person with a vested interest in the issue is 100 percent under your control, not the other persons! Changing the result is as simple or as difficult as changing your behavior. Just imagine how different your family, church, relationships, company, or even country could be if everyone took personal ownership (responsibility) for their outcomes. Maybe Gandhi was right when he said, *"We must be the change we wish to see in the world."*[1] So here's a question for you, are you happy with the outcomes you are experiencing in your life and work? In what areas would you like to see change? What have you been blaming on other people or the circumstances around you? What is it about you that is producing these kind of relational and occupational outcomes? Remember, *"In order to get what you have never gotten, you must be willing to do what you have never done."* Ownership is something that we normally don't do quickly. It often takes a lot of emotional diversion, juggling, and energy to finally say, "Ok, maybe I should look at me here!" Blaming the other person never gets to the root of the problem, it only enlarges it! Blaming only makes it more difficult to resolve a relational conflict. If conflict is the dry wood, then blaming is the match that can slowly burn away any hope for resolve! It is unrealistic to think that by diverting ownership the issue will somehow work itself out and not end up coming back to bite you! *Where there is the absence of resolve, there is the presence of resentment!* It may not manifest itself right away, but in time it will deteriorate the relationship to the point of being "paper thin!"

The Scottish physician and newspaper editor Samuel Smiles said, "*Where there is a will there is a way is an old true saying. He who resolves upon doing a thing, by that very resolution often scales the barriers to it, and secures its achievement.*"[2]  Blaming instead of owning puts a tight lid on any possibility of meaningful and authentic resolution between two or more people.  To step out and resolve to address the "blame pattern" in your life is to achieve and secure relational success both personally as well as occupationally.

"I call it The Blame Game."

The cartoon says it best. Rotating the pointing fingers and dodging ownership is shifting the blame away from you and consequently eliminating your need to take charge of your own life. This leaves the other person either to press in and try to hold you accountable for what they see as selfishness on your part, or give in and sweep it under the carpet with the other 537 issues that have never been resolved! Can you see now where the absence of resolve (The Blame Game) can eventually lead to resentment? Being courageous enough to take ownership to the degree that you may be wrong, is to witness the versatile and incredible person that you were meant to express in life!

## The Benefits of Ownership

Changes your thinking about measuring success: People measure success in many different ways. Whereas one person may view success as delegating to a team in order to get the job completed, someone else may feel that micromanaging is the way to go about it. But let's say that the department head who is micromanaging (possibly a Melancholy/Choleric) is finding that the team is resenting being scrutinized by him, in particular because they're both clear and knowledgeable about what to do and how to do it. As time goes on the DH is finding that there are people on the team that are jumping ship to other departments which leaves gaps in the job being completed.

Consequently, the DH fills the gaps with new workers but has to train them which takes more time and energy on his part. He still micromanages, eventually gets the job completed but with a team that is disgruntled and not giving 100% because of the discord that exists between the DH and themselves! The DH feels that it's worth the resentment to him by the team as long as the job gets done "his way!"

The department head's measure of success was obviously different from the teams. Again, "where there is the absence of resolve, there is the presence of resentment!" Let's cut to the chase. If this guy was willing to take some ownership here and look at how inefficient and controlling his management tactics was, his level of success may very well have increased greatly, not to mention the higher morale on the team's part! To be open enough to change your thinking if the machine isn't running properly, can give you a more efficient ruler to measure a more successful outcome.

Convert victim thinking into ownership thinking: Everyone is prone to negative, pessimistic, victim thinking at times. It is not an unusual thing to feel that you're being misunderstood or misrepresented in a conversation or in a particular issue. But when your feelings of being a victim when communicating with others seems to be the "rule" rather than "exception," then it very well may be time to rethink the way you process what you hear!

Here are some classic victim thinking sentences.

- "All churches are the same; they just want your money."
- "This would be a nicer place to work if they gave us more benefits."
- "I wouldn't respond this way if you'd only do what I'm asking."
- "Why should I consider you, you don't consider me."

You can feel that you are a victim in many areas: your job, being misunderstood, the government, the taxes you pay, modern technology, your wife or husband, the way you were raised, etc. Without realizing it, you can become prey to a victim thinking mentality that hampers your ability to be relationally successful and occupationally satisfied!

You may not be able to change the environment you are in, but you can definitely choose the kind of reaction that you give. And you can also choose to be more conscience of projecting a victim mentality, in particular if it's brought to your attention by others!

Here are four converting steps that can prove helpful in choosing ownership thinking over victim thinking when interacting with those around you.

**Want to nurture your words**. If you change your words, you can change your world! What you say, how you say it, and the way you deliver it, has an enormous effect on the conversational atmosphere that you find yourself in. Proverbs 21:23 says, *"He who guards his mouth and his tongue keeps himself from calamity."* In taking time to consider the potential fallout from a response given by you, could make the difference between a passionate evening or sleeping on the couch! Don Miguel Ruiz said, *"The word is not just a sound or a written symbol. The word is a force; it is the power you have to express and communicate, to think, and thereby to create the events of your life."*[3] To nurture what flows out of your mouth as well as the way you package and send it, has the likelihood to bring either great joy and success or frustration and failure into your life. The principle of *Approach = Response* can prove very beneficial here. The way you approach a person, that is, what you say, the words you have chosen, the way you have packaged it and sent them and the tone and body language you display, has much to do with the kind of response you'll receive. So if, in your opinion, the conversation went south, to then consider "the way" you approached the person becomes a massive step in successful ownership thinking. The relational dividend has the potential of being huge! Consider thinking of it this way, "to convert your thinking, will often keep you from sinking!"

### See mistakes as valued lessons for success.

Mistakes are not a bad thing for anyone who wants to succeed in any of the endless arenas of life. In fact, I believe that any person that is willing to evaluate their own blunders ultimately becomes a much stronger, personally effective, wiser, and successful person.

It is a powerful thing to conduct an internal post mortem to examine how your mistakes were made and how to benefit from the lessons learned. To discover the art of taking the "lemons" in your temperament and making "lemonade" has tremendous merit in achieving your desired goals in life!

Every mistake is a new challenge, but each mistake contains valuable lessons that can be applied to future encounters. What you learned can be implemented into your life's experience so as to avoid the same problems recurring down the road. Actually, every mistake opens up a potential new opportunity for success in life. By not evaluating mistakes on the journey, your chances for success become greatly diminished or even lost.

The great jazz trumpeter Miles Davis said, "*There are no mistakes, only lessons!*"[4] Making mistakes helps you to grow more effectively and sensitively. It also helps to show you what does and does not work in life. Mistakes, or lessons, can actually be used to help guide you toward a more meaningful and quality filled life. James Joyce declared, "*Mistakes are the portals of discovery.*"[5] If you really want to become aware of the components in your life that hinder relational and occupational stability, then make it your business to discover the reasoning behind your mistakes. The outcome, more often than not, is valued lessons for ongoing success and emotional stability!

**Be more open to embrace change.** When asked about his thoughts on change, President John F. Kennedy was quoted as saying, "*Change is the law of life. And those who look only to the past or present are certain to miss the future.*"[6] Without being open to new horizons of change in your life for the future, you limit your possibilities to where you find yourself today.

Most people tend to resist change. Why? The reason is simple really. Once you become comfortable with what you do and how you do it (Status Quo), you naturally find it hard to embrace something that is different (Future Potential). Change leaves a person apprehensive to launch out, fearing that they may appear less competent, effective and efficient in what they do. This is why change is often scary. Yet, it is a main ingredient to a successful life.

Work hard at disciplining yourself to override your first instinctive reaction to resist the change that is brought before you. Adopt a pioneer spirit. Look at the change not as a threat to your current standard of doing things, but as an opportunity to learn, grow and expand your capabilities!

If you want to be joyful and content and desire your life to improve in certain areas, then again, don't expect things to change, unless you make it happen! If not, then it becomes the definition for insanity, "doing the same thing everyday, expecting a different result!" Traveling the same road always leads you to the same place! If this is where you find yourself, then be open to embrace change. In the end you may find that the change you're looking at in a given situation doesn't fit well in what you're trying to accomplish. But then again, by just being open to it, you may find the door to the future!

**Realize that life isn't just about you.** In order to really be able to fully appreciate the essence of who you were designed to be, then try to pattern a life of giving more than receiving! To quote Franklin D. Roosevelt again, *"Self-interest is the enemy of all true affection."*[7] Personal success, emotional steadiness, relational stability and financial security are all well and good when put in proper perspective. Although, when you lose your ability to feel compassion and affection toward your fellow man, it all then becomes the "tail wagging the dog!" When self-gain and self-centeredness become more paramount in your life than sympathy and empathy for those who struggle around you, then it's time to take the engine apart and start again!

Inspired by the Catherine Ryan Hyde novel, "Pay It Forward," and by the film that bears the same name, seventh-grader Alex Southmayd set out on a quest to create a "give" culture rather than a "get" culture. Alex had a brainstorm and called it, "Give It Forward Today" (G.I.F.T). The mission of the G.I.F.T. Project is to inspire, motivate, and empower Humankind to take action and Give It Forward Today to their fellow human beings. Giving it forward simply means, giving "Yourself," to other fellow human beings through random acts of kindness and care.[8] It takes your mind off of you (the victim) and places it on someone else who may really be the victim!

These acts of kindness do not necessarily have to include money. Instead, they could be, visiting the sick or elderly, forgiving an estranged relationship, lending your car to a friend, or driving acquaintances to their intended destinations. But then again, some may include money. This could be buying a stranger a meal, or paying the toll fee for the car behind you. And if God has blessed you financially to the place where you can pay someone's mortgage for a month or help a student with their tuition or help some struggling family with clothing or groceries, you should consider doing it. It's about realizing that life isn't just about you. It is the heart of God to help alleviate a burden from someone if it's within your power to do so.

The gesture is both an act of selflessness as well as humility. And humility doesn't mean having to think less of yourself; it just means thinking of yourself less!

Jesus said in Luke 6:38,

> *Don't pick on people, jump on their failures, criticize*
> *their faults—unless, of course, you want the same*
> *treatment. Don't condemn those who are down; that*
> *hardness can boomerang. Be easy on people; you'll*
> *find life a lot easier. Give away your life; you'll find life*
> *given back, but not merely given back—given back with*
> *bonus and blessing. Giving, not getting is the way.*
> *Generosity begets generosity.*
> *(The Message)*

If there is ever a scripture that personifies the realization that life isn't just about you, it's Luke 6:38! Jesus sums this principle up by saying that our blessing in life will be based upon our willingness to bless others. The famous 19th century English pastor and theologian Charles H. Spurgeon said, "*A good character is the best tombstone. Those who loved you and were helped by you will remember you when forget-me-nots have withered. Carve your name on hearts, not on marble.*"[9] To convert and restructure your thinking pattern away from self-absorption and toward acts of kindness and charity for others, frees you to be an instrument of hope and inspiration to those who are desperately looking for something authentic in humanity. This is a major element of the compassionate YOU that you have been created to be and express!

The words within the "Act of Humility" prayer are good words indeed to live by when assuming ownership in your part of reaching out toward your fellow man.

> *Help me O Lord that my eyes may be merciful, so that*
> *I may never suspect or judge from appearances, but*
> *look for what is beautiful in my neighbors' soul and*
> *come to their rescue and that I may give heed to his*
> *needs, pains and moaning, and above all to have a*
> *word of comfort and forgiveness for all.*[10]

So in summery, ownership is pointing the finger of responsibility back to yourself and away from others when you are discussing the consequences of your actions. It is realizing that YOU determine your feelings and responses about any events or actions addressed to you, no matter how negative they seem. And lastly, it is acknowledging that you are solely responsible for the choices that you make in your life; this pertains to compassion toward your fellow man as well.

If ownership is placed on your back burner, yet you desire to achieve and succeed in your journey, then the words of Marshall McLuhan will most likely end up being your motto in life, "*We drive into the future using only our rear view mirror.*"[11] In other words, in your quest for a more vibrant future, you'll end up being defined much more by your mistakes of the past than by your desired accomplishments for tomorrow!

## Chapter Six

# Nourishing Your Mind and Soul

According to the American Heritage Dictionary, the word nourish means:

- To provide with food or other substances necessary for life and growth; feed.
- To foster the development of; promote.
- To keep alive; maintain: nourish a hope.[1]

Based on this definition, nourishing your mind and soul can mean finding interesting, exciting and stimulating ways to experience life, learn, grow, and change. It can also mean that not finding a way to create, experience, and grow can be detrimental to you. If your mind and soul is malnourished perhaps by wounding from your past or unhealthy choices you have made, then be of good cheer, there are ways that you can be free from that pain! To be able to build a strong body requires healthy food. The mind and soul also needs nourishment to grow healthy, vibrant and strong through your journey. Just as the body is what you eat, the mind absorbs what it experiences.

Your **mind** refers to the aspects of intellect and consciousness manifested as combinations of thought, perception, memory, emotion, will, and imagination. Your mind is the stream of your consciousness. It includes all of the brain's conscious processes.

Your mind is frequently synonymous with thought. It is the private conversation with yourself that you carry on "inside our head." Thus we "make up our minds," "change our minds," or are "of two minds" about something. Of course, if you want to take that expensive European vacation and really don't have the money to do it, then your wife may say that you're "out of your mind!" One of the key attributes of the mind then, is that it is a private place in which no one but the owner and God has access. No other human can "know you mind." They can only know what you choose to communicate to them.

Similar but yet different is your **soul**. According to many religious and philosophical traditions, your soul is the self-aware qualities or characteristics unique to a particular living being. In these traditions, the soul incorporates the inner attributes of each living being, and is to be the true basis for wisdom, morality and immortality (Heaven).

In Genesis 2:7 it reads, "*And the Lord God formed man of the dust of the ground, and breathed into his nostrils the breath of life; and man became a living being*", [nephesh] Hebrew for soul. The soul includes the conscious and subconscious minds, the realm of emotions and the will. Soul gives a man and a woman personality, self-awareness, rationality and natural feeling.

It is this "breath from God" into the body of every human being that gives you depth, definition and a natural homing device that cries out for relationship with your Heavenly Father.

## What Nourishes the Mind and Soul?

To effectively be able to discover and enjoy the freedom of being YOU, strengthening your mind and soul should become a priority! This fast paced, tech oriented, emotionally demanding, get it done quickly, look out for you first world that we live in, isn't designed to be mind and soul care friendly! Taking care of your mind and soul should lie in the balance of your life, with intense selfishness on one end, and extreme sacrificing for others on the other end.

In fact, nurturing your mind and soul is a key factor in being able to keep up strength, faith, resolve, motivation and inner resources. As a matter of fact, nourishing these important components will allow you to effectively give to others, whether that be your spouse, family and other important people in your inner circle or the larger community around you.

So how do you nourish "mind and soul care?" How about an early morning or evening walk repeating your life mantra, favorite scripture or encouraging quote? Taking time to quietly meditate or pray has both spiritual, as well as physical/emotional benefits to it. Daily meditation and scripture reflection are not only good mind and soul nurturing tools, they are also great stress and anxiety relievers!  Allowing too much to be crammed into your day without mind and soul care not only leaves you emotionally depleted, it robs you of the richness of peace that God has purposed for you to enjoy.  The Apostle John made very clear to us in 3 John 1:2 just how beneficial and balanced you should be in terms of your life responsibilities including health and the nourishing of your soul.  *"Beloved, I pray that in all respects you may prosper and be in good health, just as your soul prospers."*

Let's take a look at what it really means to "prosper!" Most often when we think of prosperity, we think of financial or material blessings.  But there are many other, dare I say, even "better" ways to prosper than by the material aspects alone. Below are four prosperity insights that have the potential to both refresh and enrich your mind and soul.

### INSIGHT ONE: Thankfulness

Regardless as to whether you feel prosperous or not, the truth is that most of us in modern Western society are tremendously prosperous, materially as well as in many other ways. All you need to do is compare your life with the struggle for survival and subsistence that most people in the world experience, and you can then begin to realize and appreciate just how truly fortunate and blessed you really are.

No matter what your individual problems or personal challenges may be, it's important to pause and take time every day to appreciate all that you have, in every aspect of life. Each of us should literally "count our blessings" and give thanks to God for what He has allowed us to enjoy and experience in terms of prosperity.

Also, try to make it your practice to express your appreciation as often as possible for the people in your life who you love and are meaningful to you. Be thankful for the many relationships that have prospered you and enhanced your life experience. Let them know in words as well as deeds just how very much they mean to you.

Another way to prosper from being thankful is to start a "thankful journal." This is really an effective tool because it keeps you focused on the gracious and wonderful things that have happened to you in your life. It helps you to both visualize and emotionally recall the blessed things that you have experienced as well as do. This tends to place your frustrations, disappointments and stressors into proper perspective. When you actually can begin to "see" the benefit from this different kind of prosperity, you can sit back in humble appreciation and give thanks for being so blessed! This mode of thankfulness offers great comfort as well as emotional and spiritual nourishing to your mind and soul.

### INSIGHT TWO: Awareness

Each one of us has certain core values, beliefs, and temperament patterns that limit our ability to experience an honest and genuine sense of prosperity. Feelings of being unworthy, fear of failure or success, negative messages planted into your psyche from childhood, anger, unforgiveness, abuse and other issues stand to block out a legitimate feeling of rest and peace for your mind and soul. The majority of these beliefs and messages are unconscious within you; you really aren't aware of them and yet they control your life more than you could possibly imagine. Although, the sooner you begin to consciously recognize them, the sooner you will be on the path to not only peace of mind and soul, but also an exciting discovery of the YOU that was meant to be expressed!

The illuminating awareness about what has and has not worked in your life experience, lays down a powerful foundation by which to build a secure place to find true and meaningful prosperity! You have to want to provide an atmosphere whereby your mind and soul is able to properly draw from. If that atmosphere is contentious or stressful, then obviously you are not providing a positive nurturing ground in order to reap good mind and soul benefits. On the other hand, if you are allowing yourself a place and time to draw from the provisions that God has made available to you, i.e., prayer, sight relaxation, temperament understanding, exercise, meditation, journaling etc., then you are nurturing proper mind and soul benefits!

Being conscious of where you have been, what you have come out of and where you want to go has a penetrating effect on your self-worth and sense of destiny! When you have become unaware of what has pulled you down and tried to define you throughout the years, then you are destined to repeat the behavior that has injured you and prohibited success on your life's journey. Consequently, your mind and soul become grieved and overloaded with lessons not learned and God intended productivity unexpressed!

## INSIGHT THREE: Setting Personal Goals

Once you have a sense of what true prosperity is all about, you can then begin to set some specific life goals for yourself. I find when I counsel or coach most people, setting goals is not always that difficult of a task. But when it comes to accomplishing those goals, well that's another story! But in reality, I find the most difficult thing for people to do when it comes to life goal setting, is not setting or even accomplishing the goal, but rather to know when to "let go" of the goal!

John Seely Brown, former Chief Scientist of Xerox Corporation said, *"The harder you fight to hold on to specific assumptions, the more likely there's gold in letting go of them."*[2] In other words, as long as you have to continue to fight to see light at the end of the tunnel, in terms of your goal, then there is a good likelihood that the light flickered out...you just don't know it or just haven't accepted it! But to know the art of when to "let go" of one goal in order to begin the next, can save you time, energy, money and an unnecessary failure mentally!

Think of the different aspects of your life that are important to you and make a list of them, example: **Career, Community Service, Faith, Education, Creativity, Family, Finances, Physical Fitness, Emotional Fitness, Mind and Soul Care etc.**

Then write down your goals in each of your specific categories and consider them very carefully. Are they realistic? Are they achievable? What is your timeline in order to accomplish each of them? Are there different timelines for different goals? What will prohibit, or prohibits, you from being able to effectively achieve your goals? How will these goals prosper you as a person that is designed to succeed in life other than just material success?   How does your goals impact and inspire the lives of those around you?

Here is where true prosperity comes into focus, because it takes the concentration off of just you and success, and places it on the greater purpose, that being *others* in their life success as well!  Plato gave us great wisdom for imparting true prosperity when he said, "*Good actions give strength to ourselves and inspire good actions in others.*"[3] When aspiring for personal goals, remember to include the goal of "others" into the mix, this is truly the gift that keeps on giving!

## INSIGHT FOUR: Sharing Your Gifts and Talents

At this point in the book, you have either come to the conclusion that you have something to offer, though you thought you didn't, or still feel that you have little to nothing to offer.  If you are the latter, stay tuned, hopefully after reading the pages ahead you'll change your mind!

Often we find it difficult to recognize and fully appreciate our own gifts and talents. The reason is because they come so naturally that they don't seem like a big deal at all. The things you find yourself naturally gravitating toward, the things you find that you just can't help doing and expressing, are clear indications of what you are here to accomplish in this life. More often than not, the things you feel passionate about are clues to your life purpose.

Ask yourself two questions, "What is it that I really like to do? What do I find myself naturally gravitating to?" For example, I personally find myself constantly sharing with people concerning their God given identity as well as becoming aware of their life purpose! I have a passion and excitement for sharing this process of life with anyone interested in listening! As a result, I've been able to counsel, coach, write, speak, and give seminars about this transforming message of personal growth for living. I didn't particularly plan this, nor could I have predicted the journey that I've found myself on. It just began to evolve as I followed my interests, faith, and desires.

Unless you have somehow blocked out your ability to succeed or receive in your life's journey, God will always reward you graciously for what you end up investing into the mix. It is in the answering of what calls you that you end up discovering as well as developing your God instilled gifts and talents. This is a great part of nourishing your mind and soul. It *keeps alive* and *promotes* the originally instilled God induced life expression that He has personally lodged within you!

# Providing a "Life Filter"

In looking for an applicable definition for the word "filter," I came across one that I thought was really cool!

> *Any of various electric, electronic, acoustic, or optical devices used to reject signals, vibrations, or radiations of certain frequencies while allowing others to pass.* [4]

I thought to myself, "Now that's a really vivid picture of how we should nourish our mind and soul!" Because life has the tendency of throwing you so many negative and emotionally draining "spit wads," it really becomes extremely important that you guard your mind and soul from these nasty attacks!

I find that one of the best ways to do this is to provide for yourself a *Life Filter*! The life filter is designed, as the definition says, to reject signals, vibrations or frequencies that have found their way into your world in order to create havoc and destruction to your life purpose! These optical devices, signals, vibrations or frequencies are everywhere on your journey. For instance, an example of an "optical" device could be the sensual glance that your female coworker throws you from time to time as to say, "Are you picking up my invitation, Charlie?" This pressure is really compounded if you happen to be married! The potential damage that this can have on your mind and soul, not to mention your marriage, is enormous if you haven't installed your life filter to catch the seductive vibrations and frequencies being thrown at you.

One way you could use your life filter, is to establish boundaries. Let's say, in this case, that you are married and finding that your subtle messages of "back off" just aren't sinking in! At the same time you are also finding that there is a little piece deep inside of you that likes the attention but yet realizes that it isn't healthy to your mind and soul to pursue the game. One life filter boundary could be to place a picture of your wife or family on your desk where the woman can clearly see it. This has a duel role. First, it sends a clear message to the woman cutting you *the eyes* that "this is my family and I love them and would do nothing to disrupt what God has given me." And second, the picture helps ground you to realize just what a responsibility you have to help cultivate and develop the marital union between you and your wife. It keeps your wife "in your head" rather than flirting with the unhealthy attention!

Another example is implementing a life filter at work where there is negative talk. Words have a lasting and embedding effect. They can either strengthen and build up or weaken and teardown a person. Your working environment has an imposing influence on your life. Remember, this is the place where you spend most of your waking hours. Therefore, if there is constant negative energy from certain people at work that seems to pull you in a direction that you don't want to go in, then break out your life filter! Try looking at these "energy zappers" as sucking life out of your mind and soul...your "calming, soothing and achieving machine!" This isn't at all to say that you are to view yourself as "above" them or more important than they are. Although, whenever there is a force that is trying to move you away from any form of life accomplishment, then it's time to make the appropriate adjustment!

In giving tips for using your God given *energy* wisely, Dr. Bob Rausch, CEO of 1 Executive Energy says, "*never park your good looking car next to a nothing to lose car, because when you have everything to lose and the other person has nothing to lose, you are in the wrong spot.*"[5] Therefore, a good life filter would be to find another place at your job where there is a more positive atmosphere or talk with the person, or persons who are negative and respectfully ask them to "chill" with all of the unproductive talk. Another possibility could be, trying to move to a different department at work or change to a different shift if you have the option of shift work. Or in a last ditch effort, you may have to look for a new place to park where there are "better looking cars"

One last example of a life filter would be in the lines of self-care. Say you have entered into a conversation with your spouse or perhaps a friend and the interaction seems to be "going south" quick! A healthy life filter would be to disengage or "unplug" from the conversation. In order to do this you may have to move to another room for a while to cool down and collect your thoughts or even take a walk, drive or listen to some soft soothing music. Once you feel that you are in a better place and have thought out what you would really like to say as well as the way you would like to say it, then re-engage with the propose of resolution. If you feel that you need more time, then your life filter could possibly be 24 hours of reflective thought and calming before re-engaging. Whatever is the case, implementing your life filter here has the great potential of "covering a multitude of sin" when it comes to productive and meaningful communication.

### Mind and Soul Boosters

Below are some great life filters that you can implement to boost as well as nourish your mind and soul.

- Strive to become more comfortable in your own skin and temperament. If not, you'll try to modify your life to be like someone else and that would be a real waste of blessed individuality!

- Stop resenting yourself and start being grateful for who you are. Begin celebrating the YOU that God purposed for this earth.

- Carve out quality time for your mind and soul to grow and be nourished, if not, the raging world around you will try to lay claim to your peace.

- Recognize and appreciate your many dimensions of gifting and talents. Refuse to be denied your God given qualities and expressions!

- Live with hope! If you are looking for peace and purpose, then there is a way to balance and nurture your life. No one can be perfect, or have a perfect life. But every one of us has the opportunity to experience perfect grace and rich mind soul nourishment through a personal relationship with the Almighty God that created you!

Many optical devices, signals, vibrations and frequencies (life's spit wads) will blast against you in many areas on your journey. But implementing the proper life filter at the right times will prove to be super valuable when Darth Vader is breathing down your neck and trying to strangle, not only your mind and soul nourishment out of you, but also your life purpose! Not implementing a life filter, robs you of the true and incredible YOU that was meant to be expressed, fulfilled and influential!

*Chapter Seven*

# Discovering the Greater You

Your temperament, talents and gifting were given to you by God as raw materials to accomplish your purpose in life. They are like planted seeds. You have to nurture them, cultivate them, water them and make them spring out from the soil to blossom and flourish. If you starve these seeds or neglect their worth, they will simply wither and die. Every human being is born with them. They are not an optional extra, but a standard issued specification.

There are things that just come naturally to you, they "flow"...you don't have to grunt and strain to make them happen. For example, you put me in a construction setting where I have to do measurements, build walls and read plans...man I'm lost in space! On the other hand, if you put me in front of 1,000 people using PowerPoint to speak to them about *identity*, I'm "movin and groovin!" There are some things in life that you really have to work at, and then there are other things that just come to you naturally!

There are so many people in life who believe they don't possess any meaningful qualities or talents. In reality that simply is not true. There is something under the sun that you are gifted at doing and displaying. If you really find that it is honestly difficult to come up with something, then take some time and sit yourself down and think very hard. If after you have done that you still feel clueless, try asking some people that you really trust and respect for their opinion on the matter. There is a *greater you* that is in there, you just have to be diligent to press in so as to *discover* areas that have been laying dormant yet waiting to burst out like a racehorse at the gate!

Peter Drucker, former writer, management consultant and university professor said of personal strengths, "*Most Americans do not know what their strengths are. When you ask them, they look at you with a blank stare, or they respond in terms of subject knowledge, which is the wrong answer.*" To discover not only your strengths, but the YOU that was meant to be brought to the forefront of your everyday life challenges and opportunities, is to give "full expression" to your purpose. It's time that you stop having the "blank stare" when thinking of just what you have been blessed with in order to make a lasting and meaningful impact in your sphere of the world!

In their book, "*Now, Discover Your Strengths,*" Marcus Buckingham and Donald O. Clifton, after extensive research and after interviewing more than 2,000,000 people, came up with two basic assumptions:

1.  Each person's talents are enduring and unique.

2.  Each person's greatest room for growth is in the
    areas of his or her greatest strengths.[2]

Most people believe that their greatest improvement will
come from overcoming their weaknesses. Buckingham and
Clifton say, NO! Your greatest improvement will come from
identifying your natural talents and strengthening them.  So how
do you go about identifying your natural talents, and I'll add
gifting here as well, and then strengthen them?  Well, aside from
taking a test such as, The Birkman Method or The Buckingham-
Clifton StrengthsFinder Profile, which are great tools to help you
determine your talents and gifting, consider doing a less expensive
"internal" evaluation first.

Try to determine your *natural talents*. You often have
abilities or skills that you excel at and may even bring you
recognition, however, not all of them qualify as your natural
strengths, gifting or talents. According to Donald Clifton, a
strength can be defined as "*a pattern of behavior, thoughts and
feelings that produce a high degree of satisfaction and pride.*" This
also helps you to better understand your *life purpose* as well.  For
example;

It <u>is</u> most likely a natural talent or strength if you:

*   do or learn it with little or no effort.
*   have a strong yearning to know more about it.

109

- feel thoroughly engaged, unaware of the passing of time when you do it.
- feel great joy and satisfaction when you do it.

It <u>is not</u> most likely a natural talent or strength if you:

- think you <u>should</u> do it.
- are good at it but don't enjoy it.
- can't wait for it to be over.
- don't seem to be getting any better at it. [3]

Let's take a look at two areas in your life that can help bring to focus both your life purpose as well as helping to discover the greater YOU.

## *Vocation*

> *where the needs of the world and your talents cross,*
> *there lies your vocation.* [4]
> *- Aristotle*

Although the word vocation has become associated with technical fields of trade and skill, the Latin root of the word means "calling." I am deliberately using this word because it connects the idea of "career" with a deeper and more meaningful desire to do *good* in your corner of the world. It implies that you are attracted to certain career paths that allow you to fulfill your individual purpose as well as express your unique gifts and talents. So the question is not so much "what do you want to be when you

grow up," but rather "what do you need or feel compelled to do?"
What is your passion and life expression! What is it that you want
to do that can also incorporate your talents, values and belief
system? When you can answer these questions, you are
beginning to envision not merely the kind of vocation that you
should be in, but more importantly, your life purpose and
expression!

## Envisioning Your Life

> A vision is not just a picture of what could be; it is an
> appeal to our better selves, a call to become something
> more. [5]
>
> - Rosa Beth Moss Kanter

According to Richard Leider, "*living in a place where you
belong, being with the people you love, doing the right work with
purpose*"[6] are elements of the total vision of your life. What kind
of life do you want? Where do you see yourself living? What is
the balance between work, family, friends, and recreation? What
are the things in life that you are passionate about? Have you
begun to tap into your "better self" or the *greater YOU*?

Try identifying with people you respect, admire, and
would like to pattern your life after. Your admiration and
connection with those people you identify with gives you
information about your own beliefs, convictions, and desires. Get

creative about the various paths your life could take. Examples include doing environmental work in Northern California, being a History professor at a small college in the Midwest, selling real-estate in Atlanta, Georgia, working with a Tele Communication company in a major city in the US, working with your local community in helping the under privileged receive food and shelter, starting a community drama company where you and others can display your theatric abilities, going on a two month missions trip teaching children how to read English as well as sharing your faith. These "fantasies" may seem unlikely to you now, however, they provide information about your interests, your purpose, and overall vision of a meaningful life. Also, try to use this information as an imaging tool to discover aspects about you that you may have overlooked concerning what you want, the way you want to do it and how you envision your life as a result of what you have chosen to do.

Consider doing these three exercises and see what you come up with.

1.    Whose life would you like to emulate? List ten qualities of this person. Describe their lives in detail. What kind of work do they do? What do they know that you want to know or learn? What is it about their lives that you respect and admire? What have they accomplished that you would like to accomplish?

2.   Describe Five Imaginary Lives. Without censoring yourself, imagine your ideal life: where do you live, what do you do, who do you do it with, etc. Indulge the fantasy!

3.   Create a collage of the life you want. Find and tear out ten to twenty images and/or words that you instinctively are attracted to and represent what you want in your life. Place the images on poster board arranged in whatever way you wish. When you have completed the collage, sit back and take a good look at it. What kind of life have you created? What values, strengths, beliefs, interests are represented in your collage?

## Character Trait Inventory

Every one of us possesses positive and negative characteristic traits. It's very important to identify all of your personal characteristic traits as you develop your vision for the person that you want to be. Make a list of the positive traits that you would like to incorporate in your personal vision, and the negative tendencies that you would like to see weeded out.

Below are eight character traits that will not only help you cast a positive and successful vision for your life, but will also help you to discover the greater YOU!

1.   **Courage** - Having the determination to do the right thing even when others don't; the strength to follow your

conscience rather than the crowd. Attempting difficult things that are worthwhile.

2. **Good Judgment** - Choosing worthy goals and setting proper priorities. Thinking through the consequences of your actions. Basing decisions on practical wisdom and good sense.

3. **Integrity** - Having the inner strength to be truthful, trustworthy, and honest in all things. Acting justly and honorably.

4. **Kindness** - Being considerate, courteous, helpful, and understanding of others. Showing care, compassion, friendship, and generosity. Treating others as you would like to be treated.

5. **Perseverance** - Being persistent in pursuit of worthy objectives in spite of difficulty, opposition, or discouragement. Exhibiting patience and having the fortitude to try again when confronted with delays, mistakes, or failures.

6. **Respect** - Showing high regard for authority, for other people, for self, for property, and for country. Understanding that all people have value as human beings.

7. **Responsibility** - Being dependable in carrying out obligations and duties. Showing reliability and consistency

in words and conduct. Being accountable for your own actions. Being committed to active involvement in your community.

8.  **Self-Discipline** - Demonstrating hard work and commitment to purpose. Regulating yourself for improvement and refraining from inappropriate behaviors. Being in proper control of your words, actions, impulses, and desires. Choosing abstinence from premarital sex, drugs, tobacco and other harmful substances and behaviors. If you drink alcohol, to do so responsibly and sparingly.

## understanding You

*A person who is alive is constantly getting lost. The big thing...is to realize that this is [your] own adventure, and that all the field guides and oracles and shamans...holding up mirrors can only flash you...a glimpse of your own story. It's yours to savor. It belongs to no one else.* [7]

*– Bonnie Friedman*

Exploring what matters to you is your job in life. In order to get a clear and concise picture of the areas that make up the person that you are, there needs to be an exploration for understanding. As you do this, you end up finding what really matters to you in life. You have a conscious awareness of why you are making your choices, insuring that they are based on your own desires, interests, talents, beliefs, and values and not someone else's.

For instance, after that augment with your wife where you were left staring into space when she said, "Why aren't you able to just share your feelings with me?", you then gravitated into the next room where you began your familiar "internalizing mode!" Try exploring just why you tend to stuff your emotions when asked to express your thoughts on a particular "feeling" related issue. You're probably thinking, "I really do want this tension to leave between my wife and me, but I also don't want to do the 'emotion thing' because I just don't do that very well and it makes me feel uncomfortable." Well, you've identified one part of understanding yourself, and that is that you at least "have a *desire*" to alleviate the tension between you two. You may ask, "Doesn't everyone have a desire to end tension?" The short answer here would be, "No!" Some people are perfectly satisfied "leaving sleeping dogs lie." It bothers them very little to not address the issue, because to them, to not address it is much less work than to face all of the emotions connected with addressing it!

Now let's check in with the *values* that you hold as important standards of quality in your life. Were there any positive messages that were imparted to you as a child that would speak to wanting resolution in marital conflict? Did you witness your parents disagree or argue about issues but end up talking and communicating about them that led to <u>resolution</u>? Or did you witness the complete opposite where issues just constantly hung out there and where seldom or never resolved within the marriage? Let's just say that it was the latter, but there is a great longing in you to not want to repeat in your marriage what you witnessed growing up as a child. Now you are beginning to understand and discover the greater YOU when it comes to what *values* are meaningful! You are now identifying certain standards of value that exist in you, things that matter and are important even though you didn't view this example growing up.

The following is a great story of a man who discovers a part of his true *belief* system and comes to understand his amazing determination under extreme pressure.

In 1883, a creative engineer named John Roebling was inspired by an idea to build a spectacular bridge connecting New York with Long Island. However bridge building experts throughout the world thought that this was an impossible feat and told Roebling to forget the idea. It just could not be done. It was not practical. It had never been done before.

Roebling could not ignore the vision he had in his mind of this bridge. He thought about it all the time and he knew deep in his heart that it could be done. He just had to share the dream with someone else. After much discussion and persuasion he managed to convince his son, Washington, an up-and-coming engineer, that the bridge in fact could be built.

Working together for the first time, the father and son developed concepts of how it could be accomplished and how the obstacles could be overcome. With great excitement and inspiration, and the headiness of a wild challenge before them, they hired their crew and began to build their dream bridge.

The project started well, but when it was only a few months underway a tragic accident on the site took the life of John Roebling. Washington was injured and left with a certain amount of brain damage, which resulted in him not being able to walk or talk or even move.

"We told them so."

"Crazy men and their crazy dreams."

"It`s foolish to chase wild visions."

Everyone had a negative comment to make and felt that the project should be scrapped since the Roeblings were the only ones who knew how the bridge could be built. In spite of his handicap Washington was never discouraged and still had a burning desire to complete the bridge and his mind was still as sharp as ever.

He tried to inspire and pass on his enthusiasm to some of his friends, but they were too daunted by the task. As he lay on his bed in his hospital room, with the sunlight streaming through the windows, a gentle breeze blew the flimsy white curtains apart and he was able to see the sky and the tops of the trees outside for just a moment.

It seemed that there was a message for him not to give up. Suddenly an idea hit him. All he could do was move one finger and he decided to make the best use of it. By moving this, he slowly developed a code of communication with his wife.

He touched his wife's arm with that finger, indicating to her that he wanted her to call the engineers again. Then he used the same method of tapping her arm to tell the engineers what to do. It seemed foolish but the project was under way again.

For 13 years Washington tapped out his instructions with his finger on his wife's arm, until the bridge was finally completed. Today the spectacular Brooklyn Bridge stands in all its glory as a tribute to the triumph of one man's indomitable spirit and his determination not to be defeated by circumstances. It is also a tribute to the engineers and their teamwork, and to their faith in a man who was considered mad by half the world. It stands too, as a tangible monument to the love and devotion of his wife who for 13 long years patiently decoded the messages of her husband and told the engineers what to do.[8]

Perhaps this is one of the best examples of a never-say-die attitude that overcomes a terrible physical handicap and achieves

an impossible goal. Washington Roeblings had no idea
whatsoever of the unbelievable determination that existed within
him.  It was only under extreme pressure that this quality was able
to rise to the top.  He, as well as many others, came to discover
the greater implanted abilities and inspiration that was lodged
deep within the recesses of his inner most being.  So often you
don't know who you really are until the going gets tough!   The
greater YOU pops out when you least expect it.  This was
Washington Roebling's story, it was his "adventure" being
unveiled before his very eyes.  His raw tenacity was a diamond in
the rough.  His strong beliefs were hidden; they were there all of
the time but just had to be squeezed in order to bring his vision to
the forefront.  His vision was "an appeal to [his] better self, a call
to becoming something more."  It is the same with you, me and
everyone else.  In order to properly and effectively envision your
life for success, there has to be a deeper call to the greater YOU!
If not, your better self will never really be expressed, and your
true potential never discovered.  The rock group, Kansas, put it
best when they said, "*I close my eyes, only for a moment, and the
moments gone.  All my dreams pass before my eyes, a curiosity.
Dust in the wind, all they are is dust in the wind.*"[9]  Remember,
it's "your own story, it's yours to savor...it belongs to no one else"
so reach out and grab it and refuse to allow any obstacle to come
against your assigned destiny for a greater YOU!

## Chapter Eight

# You and Dreaming Dreams

*"There's no use trying," Alice said.*
*"One can't believe impossible things."*
*"I daresay you haven't had much practice," said the*
*Queen. "When I was your age, I always did it for half-*
*an-hour a day. Why, sometimes I've believed as many*
*as six impossible things before breakfast."* [1]
*-Lewis Carroll (Alice's Adventures In Wonderland)*

Below is the story of a man, who under extremely difficult circumstances, dreamed of what many during his time thought was not possible.

Second Lieut. Bill Wilson didn't think twice when the first butler he had ever seen offered him a drink. The 22-year-old soldier didn't think about how alcohol had destroyed his family. He didn't think about the Yankee temperance movement of his childhood or his loving fiancée, Lois Burnham, or his emerging talent for leadership. He didn't think about anything at all. "I had found the elixir of life," he wrote. Wilson's last drink, 17 years later, when alcohol had destroyed his health and his career, precipitated an epiphany that would change his life and the lives

121

of millions of other alcoholics. Incarcerated for the fourth time at Manhattan's Towns Hospital in 1934, Wilson had a spiritual awakening — a flash of white light, a liberating awareness of God — that led to the founding of Alcoholics Anonymous and Wilson's revolutionary 12-step program, the successful remedy for alcoholism. The 12 steps have also generated successful programs for eating disorders, gambling, narcotics, debting, sex addiction, and people affected by other addictions. Aldous Huxley called him "the greatest social architect of our century."

William Griffith Wilson grew up in a quarry town in Vermont. When he was 10, his hard-drinking father headed for Canada, and his mother moved to Boston, leaving the sickly child with her parents. As a soldier, and then as a businessman, Wilson drank to alleviate his depression and to celebrate his Wall Street success. Married in 1918, he and Lois toured the country on a motorcycle and appeared to be a prosperous, promising young couple. By 1933, however, they were living on charity in her parents' house on Clinton Street in Brooklyn, New York. Wilson had become an unemployable drunk who disdained religion and even panhandled for cash. Inspired by a friend who had stopped drinking, Wilson went to meetings of the Oxford Group, an evangelical society founded in Britain by Pennsylvanian Frank Buchman. And as Wilson underwent a barbiturate-and-belladonna cure called "purge and puke," which was state-of-the-art alcoholism treatment at the time, his brain spun with phrases from Oxford Group meetings, Carl Jung and William James' "Varieties of Religious Experience," which he read in the hospital. Five sober months later, Wilson went to Akron, Ohio, on business. The deal fell through, and he wanted a drink. He stood in the lobby of the Mayflower Hotel, entranced by the sounds of the bar across the hall. Suddenly he became convinced that by helping another alcoholic, he could save himself.

Through a series of desperate telephone calls, he found Dr. Robert Smith, a skeptical drunk whose family persuaded him to give Wilson 15 minutes. Their meeting lasted for hours. A month later, Dr. Bob had his last drink, and that date, June 10, 1935, is the official birthday of A.A., which is based on the idea that only an alcoholic can help another alcoholic. "Because of our kinship in suffering," Bill wrote, "our channels of contact have always been charged with the language of the heart."

The Burnham house on Clinton Street became a haven for drunks. "My name is Bill W., and I'm an alcoholic," he told assorted houseguests and visitors at meetings. To spread the word, he began writing down his principles for sobriety. Each chapter was read by the Clinton Street group and sent to Smith in Akron for more editing. The book had a dozen provisional titles, among them "The Way Out" and "The Empty Glass." Edited to

123

400 pages, it was finally called "Alcoholics Anonymous," and this became the group's name.

But the book, although well reviewed, wasn't selling. Wilson tried unsuccessfully to make a living as a wire-rope salesman. A.A. had about a hundred members, but many were still drinking. Meanwhile, in 1939, the bank foreclosed on the Clinton Street house, and the couple began years of homelessness, living as guests in borrowed rooms and at one point staying in temporary quarters above the A.A. clubhouse on 24th Street in Manhattan. In 1940 John D. Rockefeller Jr. held an A.A. dinner and was impressed enough to create a trust to provide Wilson with $30 a week — but no more. The tycoon felt that money would corrupt the group's spirit.

Then, in March 1941, *The Saturday Evening Post* published an article on A.A., and suddenly thousands of letters and requests poured in. Attendance at meetings doubled and tripled. Wilson had reached his audience. In *Twelve Traditions,* Wilson set down the suggested bylaws of Alcoholics Anonymous. In them, he created an enduring blueprint for an organization with a maximum of individual freedom and no accumulation of power or money. Public anonymity ensured humility. No contributions were required; no member could contribute more than $1,000.

Today more than 2 million A.A. members in 150 countries hold meetings in church basements, hospital conference rooms, and school gyms, following Wilson's informal structure. Members identify themselves as alcoholics and share their stories; there are no rules or entry requirements, and many members use only first names.

Wilson believed the key to sobriety was a change of heart. The suggested 12 steps include an admission of powerlessness, a moral inventory, a restitution for harm done, a call to service, and a surrender to a personal God. Influenced by A.A., the American Medical Association has redefined alcoholism as a chronic disease, not a failure of willpower.

As Alcoholics Anonymous grew, Wilson became its principal symbol. He helped create a governing structure for the program, the General Service Board, and turned over his power. "I have become a pupil of the A.A. movement rather than the teacher," he wrote. He was always Bill W., refusing to take money for counseling and leadership. Wanting to draw no attention to himself, he also turned down many honors, including a degree from Yale.

Bill Wilson had a dream for those struggling with alcohol addiction, and that dream was to have available a program for help that would be free of charge and filled with hope! Through many trials, setbacks, and discouragements, Bill W. stubbornly refused to lay down his dream of helping those shackled by substance abuse. His dream was birthed through adversity and thrives today in helping untold millions have a chance at facing life's potential through acknowledging their powerlessness over their addictions.[2]

## Moses the Dreamer

In his book, *Overcoming Life's Disappointments*, Rabbi Harold S. Kushner, shows us how to be our best selves even when things don't turn out as we had hoped. It shows how we can overcome life's disappointments as well as dare to dream! Kushner turns to the experience of Moses to find the essential lessons of strength and faith. Moses towers over all others in the Old Testament: he is the man on the mountaintop to whom God speaks with unparalleled intimacy, and he leads his people out of bondage. But he is also deeply human, someone whose soaring triumphs are offset by frustration and longing: his people ignore his teachings, he is denied entrance to the Promised Land, his family suffers, but he overcomes through his faith and his endless yearning to dream!

From the life of Moses, Kushner gleans principles that can help us deal with the problems we encounter through life's journey. Through the example of Moses' remarkable resilience, we learn how to weather the disillusionment of dreams unfulfilled, the pain of a lost job or promotion, a child's failures, divorce or abandonment, and illness. We learn how to meet all disappointments with faith in our God-given abilities and gifting and how to respond to heartbreak with understanding rather than bitterness and despair.[3]

> *What happens to a dream deferred?*
> *Does it dry up like a raisin in the sun?*[4]

In these lines, the poet Langston Hughes wonders what happens to dreams that don't come true. I wonder what happens to the dreamer. How do people cope with the realization that important dimensions of their lives will not turn out as they hoped they would? A person's marriage isn't all he or she anticipated. Someone doesn't get the promotion or the recognition he had set his heart on. Many of us look at the world and see two groups of people, winners and losers: those who get what they want out of life and those who don't. But in reality life is more complicated than that. Nobody gets everything he or she yearns for. I look at the world and see three sorts of people: those who dream boldly even as they realize that a lot of their dreams will not come true, those who dream more modestly and fear that even their modest dreams may not be realized, and those who are afraid to dream at all, lest they be disappointed.

History is written by winners, so most history books are about people who win. Most biographies, excluding works of pure scholarship, are meant to inspire as much as to inform, so they focus on a person's successes. But in real life, even the most successful people see some of their efforts fail and even the greatest of people learn to deal with failure, rejection, bereavement, and serious illness.

When we think of Moses, we think of his triumphs: leading the Israelites out of slavery, splitting the Red Sea, ascending Mount Sinai to receive the tablets of the law. But Moses was a man who knew frustration and failure in his public and personal life at least as often and as deeply as he knew fulfillment, and we, whose lives are also a mix of fulfillment and disappointment, can learn from his experiences. If he could overcome his monumental disappointments, you can learn to overcome yours. Through all of these setbacks, Moses continued to dream of a people free from the tyranny of a cruel dictator as well as the owners of their own promised land!

We may think that we know about Moses, if not from Sunday School classes, then perhaps from one of the movies about his life. If we do, chances are that we assign that knowledge to the dusty corner of our consciousness reserved for old Sunday School lessons, entertaining and probably edifying, but not that relevant to our daily lives. But he was not only the man on the mountaintop, the man to whom God spoke with unparalleled intimacy, but also Moses the human being, a man whose soaring triumphs were offset by crushing defeats in some of the things that mattered most to him, a man who came to realize the price his family paid for his successes. He was a hero to admire and learn from, maybe even more heroic when the all-too-human qualities of longing, frustration, regret, and resiliency have been added to the portrait. He believed against all odds and as a result, God honored his faith. Though he didn't enter it himself, the Promised Land nonetheless became a reality to millions of Israelites as a result of a dreamer who, by faith, dared to dream his dreams!

## They Say I'm a Dreamer

The greatest triumphs in business frequently begin as far-fetched goals and wild dreams! When the public first heard about a contraption that would fly people through the air like birds, many thought it was impractical, not to mention impossible. When Frederick Smith submitted his idea for an overnight delivery service to his professor at Yale, he barely got a passing grade. In 1974, it looked as though Fred Smith's dream of a worldwide overnight delivery system was about to go up in flames. His family's capital was spent, the bank loans were due, and the demand for a service of this kind was still unproven. But Smith hung on, and subsequent developments in the world economy proved him right even though they said he was just a dreamer! *"We'd run out of money and we didn't have all of the regulatory requirements that we needed. My half-sisters were up in arms because it looked like we were going to lose some money. Everything was going wrong, except the fundamentals of the business were proving every single day that the idea was right."*[5] But by adamantly continuing on a path others considered to be a dead end, Fred Smith founded FedEx.

Today, few in the business world could imagine getting along without an overnight delivery system like Federal Express. FedEx drop boxes and FedEx trucks are a familiar part of the American landscape, and FedEx planes circle the globe delivering everything from chocolates to airplane parts. To dare to dream is risky, but to not dream is to muzzle not only your creative juices, but also the possibility of great good for others!

### Dare to Dream Your Dreams

When it comes to dreamers, they often focus on the small projects that make only modest advances toward accomplishing their goals. For example, those who are entrepreneurs or aspiring entrepreneurs are at their best when they are able to challenge themselves. Being committed to achieving a big, seemingly impossible goal can reconnect you to the passion that first kick-started your dream. The process of working through a challenging idea helps you uncover inventive ways to move your dream to new and exciting levels step by step. Below are four construction truths that will help you to build your dream on a more solid and capable foundation.

1. **Choose your "mission impossible."** Create a list of one or more dream projects that you would love to complete. Progress is best achieved with clear direction, so choose an idea that will add life and interest to your dream, business or otherwise, and then connect that with your passion. Treat it as an opportunity for adventure.

2. **Define your dreams outcome by what you want to learn and give out, not just by financial results.** Keeping your mind focused on achieving a large goal should compel you to keep up with the latest trends and methods involved with making your dream a reality. These insights can inspire and assist you in transforming your dream and attaining your goals. Eliminate any reservations you have about your personal limitations by focusing on what you will learn and give out to others rather than how much money you will generate if indeed your dream is financially related.

131

3. **Make true progress on a regular basis.** Rome wasn't built in a day, but planners and workers made progress each day and the city became great as a result. Consequently, set aside a specific time each day to work on your dream. This would mean setting realistic daily goals that will help you to move closer to accomplishing your dream. Spending time on your project isn't about developing a specific plan so much as it's about the process of discovery that lays a road brick by brick that eventually leads to your finished dream. Start your journey by committing your dream to paper and making a list of questions you will need to answer to accomplish your objective.

4. **Track what you learn and don't look back.** You won't achieve your dream in one giant leap. In fact, you may find yourself taking two steps forward and one step back. Rather than being apprehensive about what may happen, embrace any setbacks you encounter and consider them learning opportunities. Use your imagination to find ways to turn each new idea into a growth strategy for your dream goals. This steady stream of accomplishments will prepare you for the day when your dream becomes a reality!

When describing people of optimism, Mark Twain once said, "*Optimist: Day-dreamer more elegantly spelled.*"[6] Unless you give yourself the liberty to dream possibilities in your life's spiritual, relational, and occupational journey, you will never really come to understand or appreciate a big part of who you are. You may not be a Moses, Bill Wilson, or Fred Smith, but you can and should be YOU! What made these men unique was both their ability and desire to believe that what has not yet happened could happen! This separated them from the status quo and caused them to stand out in a sea of mediocrity. To not be you in dreaming your dreams is to greatly minimize the Divine investment that has been placed in you. A dream is a desire or achievement that is longed for, a deep aspiration of purpose that won't leave you alone or go away! It latches on to you with a mighty grip and pulls you in the direction of its fury! No dreamer is ever too small, no dream is ever too big! So in the words of Aerosmith...

*Dream on, dream on*
*Dream yourself a dream come true*
*Dream on, dream on*
*Dream until your dream comes true...*[7]

## Chapter Nine

# You and Lighting the Darkness

*...because of the tender mercy of our God, by which*
*the rising sun will come to us from heaven to shine on*
*those living in darkness and in the shadows of death, to*
*guide our feet into the path of peace. - Luke 1:78-79*
*(NAS)*

Zacharias prophesied these words in reference to his son, John the Baptist and the ministry that he was called to do regarding his "preparing the way" for the Messiah, Jesus Christ who would deliver mankind from darkness. As I've pondered this scripture throughout the years as a former pastor, I couldn't help but to feel that each and every one of us have been called, in some way, to light the darkness around us as we identify darkness. Unlike Christ who came to address the darkness of sin and the hope of Eternity, we on the other hand have a responsibility to address, and even light up, the darkness as disciples of a more compassionate lifestyle toward our follow man. This puts into perspective the total of the person that you are and were meant to express in this life! The ravages of darkness in your sphere of community could be poverty, homelessness, hunger, bereavement, injustice, abuse, loneliness, bitterness, oppression, unforgiveness, etc. Each of us have access to a torch that is able to *light the darkness* and bring a dimension of compassion, care and even, hope to those in desperate need of rescuing, if from nothing else, themselves! If you become self-absorbed by just *your* wants, *your* desires, *your* achievements, *your* goals, and *your* attainment, then you have totally missed the mark on just who you really are and what you were really meant to express as a successful and influential creation designed by the Creator!

Let's take a look at a few everyday torchbearers and their commitment to seeing darkness dwindle from within their power to do good!

## Small Candles

Hazel Aicken well remembers her fear during June 1995 that the IRA ceasefire was about to collapse. "We just knew something was going to happen—tensions were building and building." As Vice Chair of Women Together at the time, Hazel wanted to be ready with a powerful way to show the world that Northern Ireland's people wanted peace. An artist, she visualized thousands of people taking to the streets, waving white paper doves. Women Together produced 3,000 doves. Seven months later, in February, the doves were put to use as Hazel's fear came true.

Five years ago, Hazel was a struggling community development worker in Belfast. Deeply disillusioned, she moved to a country farm and cut off her 20-year involvement with community work. It was a total escape. For two years she recuperated by painting and gardening until "I got a very powerful stirring. Something had started to move again." She accompanied a friend to a Women Together meeting and came home in shock. "I'd been nominated to go to Caux, MRA's international centre in Switzerland, to attend a conference for 'Creators of Peace.' I had never even heard of Caux!"

While there in August 1994, Hazel and Women Together Co-ordinator Anne Carr received word of the brutal sectarian murder of a pregnant mother in front of her five children. Hazel was devastated. I said, "God, I don't know why you sent me here. Whatever you want me to do, I'll do it."

A friend then showed her a video of Solzhenitsyn's Nobel Prize address. "It depicts art being used to show evil and pain and corruption. I'd always thought of art as showing the beautiful things. Suddenly I realized it didn't have to be like that." Instead of a nature scene as she normally would have done, she painted a death scene—the death of the mother. Her next painting of candles, open hands and a sun surrounded by a crown of thorns portrayed hope in God's light.

She returned home sensing God had big plans in store. "All I knew was that my life would change." Concerned about the victims of the conflict in Northern Ireland, she decided to open the farm where she lives to a cross-community group of bereaved families and individuals called Lifeline. Although a Protestant living in "a very strong traditional Unionist place," she refused to watch the annual Protestant parades on July 12 to celebrate William III's victory at the Battle of the Boyne. Instead, she invited Catholic and Protestant victims to the farm for hay rides and fun. The farm has now developed into a place of "healing and relaxation" where bereavement support groups bring victims on day trips. Her landlady eagerly joins in, and the two are members of a group who plan to convert the derelict farm mill into a residential centre where bereaved families can have a break.

Hazel did not stop there. Last Christmas she initiated Northern Ireland's first adult nativity, which took place, naturally, on the farm. Catholic and Protestant members of the local community acted out the Christmas story to a crowd of around 300. "We even had to audition the donkey!" she laughs. "I wanted a cross-community project and I wanted worship. People from both sides of the community came.". "It's just a tiny wee thing," she says, "but if there were more small candles, the darkness would lessen."[1]

# Bearers of Light and Refuge

The Rushdoonys, residents of Danville, California, founded the Macedonian Outreach organization. Vula Rushdoony was born in Greece and moved to the United States alone when she was a teenager. Haig Rushdoony is a first-generation American born to Armenian parents.

When the Rushdoonys retired, they prayed to God to give them a mission to help others. When the Rushdoonys visited Vula's cousin in Bulgaria and glimpsed the poverty-stricken lives of gypsy children and refugees, they knew they found their mission. "I just saw myself all over again," she said.

The Christian couple, members of Community Presbyterian Church in Danville, CA, has since devoted their lives to the cause. They now spend from May to September overseas each year. Macedonian Outreach serves countries such as Greece, Romania, Bulgaria, Albania, and Serbia, among others. The organization has four types of needs that they help provide to the less fortunate: spiritual, medical, educational, and everyday physical needs. They work with pastors in those countries to minister and to help people that are far less fortunate than they are. Macedonian Outreach helps provide medication, equipment and supplies for medical care, as well as sending patients who need operations to America or Western Europe. Basic needs such as food, clothing, and shelter are provided. The organization pays for children to attend school and covers the costs for supplies as well.

Haig and Vula Rushdoony know what it feels like to "light the darkness" and see first hand what a difference two people can make when tapping into the greater you![2]

## Becoming the Hands of God

In 1865 William Booth, a London minister, gave up the comfort of his pulpit and decided to take his message into the streets where it would reach the poor, the homeless and the hungry. As a result of this compassionate minister's vision to reach out to the unfortunate and the destitute, The Salvation Army was born.

His original aim was to send converts to established churches of the day, but soon he realized that the poor did not feel comfortable or welcome in the pews of most of the churches and chapels of Victorian England. Regular churchgoers were appalled when these shabbily dressed, unwashed people came to join them in worship. Booth decided to found a church especially for them — the East London Christian Mission. The mission grew slowly, but Booth's faith in God remained undiminished. In 1878 the church was renamed The Salvation Army.

By the 1900s, the Army had spread around the world. The Salvation Army soon had officers and soldiers in 36 countries, including the United States of America. This well-organized yet flexible structure inspired a great many much needed services: women's social work, the first food depot, the first day nursery, and the first Salvation Army missionary hospital. During World War II, The Salvation Army operated 3,000 service units for the armed forces, which led to the formation of the USO.

Aside from their many homeless shelters, mission outreaches and food and clothing programs, The Salvation Army also helps light the darkness through providing free health care within the many countries of Africa, The Americas and The Caribbean, South Asia, South Pacific, and East Asia. All in all, The Salvation Army provides both ministry and humanitarian help in over 106 nations around the world.

William Booth once said, "Prayer must be matched with Action." He went on to say, "If it is true that Satan trembles when he sees the weakest saint upon their knees...it is also true that Satan trembles much more when, having said his prayers, that same saint rolls up his sleeves and sets out to answer them." This is "love in action!" To answer the call of helping to light the darkness in your sphere of influence, in your little corner of the world, is to discover a wonderful and compassionate side of just who you really are and were meant to be![3]

## Provider of Hope and Encouragement

In 1999, at the annual Business for Social Responsibility Conference in Boston, a virtually unknown businessman named David Morris, from Rossville, Georgia, stood before executives from The Gap, American Express, and other major corporations and explained why his company has been so successful. "Simple," he said, "I hire the people no one else wants to hire."

As CEO of Habitat International, Inc., a major supplier of artificial grass putting greens, accent rugs, and indoor-outdoor mats for Lowes, Home Depot, and other retailers, Morris knows better than most how to work with people with special needs. After all he's been doing it for almost two decades.

Today, in a 50,000 square-foot former chicken hatchery with whimsical sculptures, a basketball court, and an employee-run radio station, three of every four Habitat workers (there are 70 during peak production) has a physical or mental disability, or both. People with schizophrenia drive forklifts next to those with Down syndrome, autism, and cerebral palsy. Recovering alcoholics, deaf employees, and homeless people cut floor runners alongside co-workers who have suffered strokes, severe head injuries, or loss of an arm. All are cross-trained on every task in the plant.

Morris is convinced that his business, which has tripled its sales since 2001, even in the economic downturn, flourishes not in spite of, but because of the company's loyal, disabled workers. And he's determined to share that message with others.

Since his appearance at the BSR conference, 47 year old Morris has helped entrepreneurs and human resources managers from across the country including a major competitor with 6,200 employees, to set up their own programs to hire people with disabilities. He has shared his humanitarian message with legislators, business peers, and community groups from Maine to Seattle, and has won numerous awards for his commitment to helping those with "distractions" to receive, not just employment, but also hope and encouragement![4]

## Doctor of Mercy

In a dusty, open-air treatment center in Savelugu, Ghana, where patients are crying in pain, Dr. Donald R. Hopkins once again meets his enemy: Guinea worm disease.

For thousands of years, the worms, which grow to a yard in length, have tormented the people of Africa and central Asia, spreading through larvae in the water and growing inside people's bodies before bursting into the open from blisters on the skin. Slowly the worms emerge, inch by painful inch, from the tiny feet of children, the eye sockets of adults or even the abdomens of pregnant women.

For nearly three decades, Hopkins, a 65 year-old Chicago physician, has fought the scourge, chasing it across the savannas of Africa and down the muddy rivers of India. He has stamped it out in 11 countries. Now, with fewer than 25,000 cases left--down from 3.5 million in 1986--Hopkins stands ready to strike the final blow, making Guinea worm the only disease in history other than smallpox to be successfully eradicated. But in this moment, Hopkins sees that he has lost a battle.

The Savelugu center was described as a scene out of hell. Flies buzz through the air and, all around him, patients scream. A woman winces as a 2 foot-long worm as thin and white as dental floss emerges from her breast. And a girl in a pink dress cries in terror as a worker pulls six inches of stringy worm from her tiny finger.

It is a plague of biblical proportions. But the doctor does not flinch. He wipes his forehead and slowly kneels beside another crying child, who looks no more than 3. The girl sobs as a worm--fully 3 feet long--is pulled from her foot. Hopkins gently pats her back, and in a soft voice, barely audible above the sounds of suffering, whispers, "It's OK. It's OK." Tomorrow, he will resume his struggle against the horrifying epidemic. Today, it is enough to comfort a crying child, to tell her that she is safe.

This is the story of one man's quest to rid the world of a tormenting disease, the story of a black man who grew up in the

144

segregated South with the dream of becoming a doctor. Dr. Hopkins, has been knighted in Mali, and presented with a horse in Niger. Two areas in Nigeria named him an honorary chief, and townspeople there dubbed him "Redeemer of Less Privileged" and "Healer of the World."

The people mentioned in this chapter are normal, everyday individuals who decided that there was more to them then just their own personal wants and aspirations in life. They reached out into the darkness with the torch that had been given to them. They may not have known that they possessed such a light, but they paused just long enough out of their busy lives to listen to the "still small voice" that directed them away from themselves and toward the cries of the destitute and wounded souls that are so loved by God![5]

Albert Schweitzer said, *"Even if it's a little thing, do something for those who have need of help, something for which you get no pay but the privilege of doing it."*[6] Do you want to know the depths of who you really are? Do you really want to be free to be the YOU that was intended to shine on this earth? Do you really want to know the impact and influence you were chosen to exhibit? Well then in the midst of your life's journey, consider incorporating time to stop and "listen" to the voice of God that says, *"...to the extent that you did it to one of the least of my brothers, you did it to Me."* (Matthew 25:40, ASV)

145

*Lord, make me an instrument of thy peace.*

*Where there is hatred let me - show love*

*Where there is injury - pardon*

*Where there is doubt - faith*

*Where there is despair - hope*

*Where there is darkness - light*

*Where there is sadness - joy*

*O, Divine Master,*

*Grant that I may not so much seek*

*To be consoled - as to console*

*To be understood - as to understand,*

*To be loved - as to love*

*For it is in giving - that we receive,*

*It is in pardoning, that we are pardoned,*

*It is in dying - that we are born to eternal life.*[7]

*- Francis of Assisi (1181-1226)*

*Chapter Ten*

# You and Discouragement

If you haven't already experienced it, do know that everyone will have their share of discouragement at some point in their lifetime. However, the way you choose to face, approach and manage your discouragement will make the difference between an emotionally successful journey and a crippled one.

The dictionary defines discouragement as follows: "*a feeling of despair in the face of obstacles; or a state of distraught and loss of sense of enthusiasm, drive or courage.*"[1]

Discouragement can happen in all areas of life. An employee puts out 110% to ensure his department achieves the goals that were set for success, only to get little or no recognition for all his hard work. Parents find out that their 16 year old daughter is pregnant! They truly feel the pangs of discouragement. A couple suffers their second miscarriage while trying to have a family. After a small business owner does everything he possibly can to keep his company going, he comes to the sad conclusion that he has to shut the doors. She was confident that her job promotion was in the bag only to find out that she was passed over by someone who was related to the department head. All of these people deal with discouragement differently; some are affected more seriously than others.

Rick Warren, pastor of Saddleback Church in Lake Forest California offers the following information regarding discouragement. [2]

## WHAT CAUSES DISCOURAGEMENT?

### 1 - FATIGUE

When you're physically or emotionally exhausted, you're a prime candidate to be infected with discouragement. Your defenses are lowered and things can seem bleaker than they really are. This often occurs when you're halfway through a major project and you get tired.

### 2 - FRUSTRATION

When unfinished tasks pile up, it's natural to feel overwhelmed. And when trivial matters or the unexpected interrupt you and prevent you from accomplishing what you really need to do, your frustration can easily produce discouragement.

### 3 - FAILURE

Sometimes, your best laid plans fall apart -- the project collapses -- the deal falls through -- no one shows up to the event. How do you react? Do you give in to self-pity? Do you blame others? As one man said, "Just when I think I can make ends meet -- somebody moves the ends!" That's discouraging!

4 - FEAR

Fear is behind more discouragement than we'd like to admit. The fear of criticism (What will they think?), the fear of responsibility (What if I can't handle this?), and the fear of failure (What if I blow it?) can cause a major onset of the blues.

## WHAT'S THE CURE FOR DISCOURAGEMENT?

There's a fascinating story in the Bible about how a guy named Nehemiah mobilized the residents of Jerusalem to build a wall around the entire city. Half way through the project, the citizens became discouraged and wanted to give up -- because of the FOUR causes I've given.

Here's what Nehemiah taught about defeating discouragement (Nehemiah 4):

### 1 - REST YOUR BODY

If you need a break – take one! You'll be more effective when you return to work. If you're burning the candle at both ends, you're not as bright as you think!

### 2 - REORGANIZE YOUR LIFE

Discouragement doesn't necessarily mean you are doing the wrong thing. It may just be that you are doing the right thing in the wrong way. Try a new approach. Shake things up a little.

### 3 - REMEMBER GOD WILL HELP YOU

Just ask Him. He can give you new energy. There is incredible motivating power in faith.

### 4 - RESIST THE DISCOURAGEMENT

Fight back! Discouragement is a choice. If you feel discouraged, it's because you have chosen to feel that way. No one is forcing you to feel bad. Hang on! Do what's right in spite of your feelings. And remember, no feeling lasts forever...there is light at the end of the tunnel!

## *Letter to George Latham*

Abraham Lincoln wrote this now classic letter of encouragement to George Latham, a close friend of his son Robert. Both boys had been raised in Springfield, Illinois, attended Phillips Exeter Academy in New Hampshire, and were Harvard hopefuls. Several months later, both would travel with the president-elect on his inaugural journey. Robert eventually graduated from Harvard, while George studied at Yale for two years. The letter reveals Lincoln's concern for a discouraged young man whose father died several years before, as well as his own passion for education and determination to persevere even through discouraging times. At first glance, the pain referred to seems overstated, but probably not to a man who carved out his own education and lacked the finances to attend prep school or college. Let's use Mr. Lincoln's letter as a template for looking at YOU and discouragement.

*Springfield, Ills. July 22, 1860*
*My dear George*

    *I have scarcely felt greater pain in my life than on learning yesterday from Bob's letter that you failed to enter Harvard University. And yet there is very little in it, if you will allow no feeling of discouragement to seize, and prey upon you. It is a certain truth, that you can enter, and graduate in, Harvard University; and having made the attempt, you must succeed in it. "Must" is the word.*

    *I know not how to aid you, save in the assurance of one of mature age, and much severe experience, that you can not fail, if you resolutely determine, that you will not.*

*The President of the institution can scarcely be other than a kind man; and doubtless he would grant you an interview, and point out the readiest way to remove, or overcome, the obstacles which have thwarted you.*

    *In your temporary failure there is no evidence that you may not yet be a better scholar*

*and a more successful man in the great struggle of*
*life, than many others, who have entered college*
*more easily.*

*Again I say let no feeling of*
*discouragement prey upon you, and in the end*
*you are sure to succeed.*

*With more than a common interest I*
*subscribe myself Very truly your friend,*
*-Abraham Lincoln*

When you really dissect President Lincoln's letter, three things jump out when looking at YOU, discouragement and its attack on your desired goals in life.[3]

## FIRST: DISCOURAGEMENT DOESN'T SPELL DEFEAT

("*It is a certain truth, that you can enter, and graduate in, Harvard University; and having made the attempt, you must succeed in it. 'Must' is the word.*")

Just because you find yourself in a disappointing situation, or even condition, that doesn't have to spell defeat in your attempt to achieve your life goal. Take a look at Sean Plasse's journey with Dyslexia and how he overcame his discouragement with it.

"A parrot flies along, the parrot lands on a car, the car explodes, and the smoke and feathers rise in a figure 8." To many people, that may sound like a cartoon panel. To Sean Plasse, it was a tool for recalling the word "polycarbonate."

Plasse suffers from dyslexia. He is able to understand and recall concepts and ideas very well. But words are another matter.

Trying to cope with his problem in college, Plasse says, he would "convert about 10,000 words into these pictures, every semester" -- and live in fear that someone would realize that he had to work so hard to keep up.

When Plasse entered the working world, with a job at a marketing company, things only got worse. In addition to working late nights, Plasse would come in on the weekends to pour over e-mails, circling problem words so he could understand what the notes were about.

Speaking recently to his friend Blanche Podhajski, Plasse recalls the difficulty and discouragement he had in keeping names straight, even after a year at the company -- and even when the names were those of the company's owners. His solution: He kept a stack of business cards on hand, referring to them when he needed to know someone's name.

"When you struggle with a learning disability," Plasse says, "it affects everything in your life."

But one day, Plasse came across an article about elite businessmen who had successfully coped with their own learning disabilities. The article, in Fortune magazine, sent Plasse to the phone book, looking for help.

After a full day of tests at a learning-disorders center, Plasse received a stark summary of his abilities -- and his challenges.

"Your IQ is in the 99th percentile," the people at the center told him. "But your ability to read and decode words is in the 14th percentile."

The news, Plasse says, changed his life. "I got in my pickup truck and cried all the way home. It was a turning point."

After working with Podhajski at the Stern Center, a literacy group in Williston, Vermont, Plasse, 31, learned to overcome his discouragement as well as fear of reading. And with a new set of learning tools, he now has his own business: Plasse Contracting.[4]

## SECOND: DETERMINATION GIVES BIRTH TO SUCCESS

*("...you can not fail, if you resolutely determine, that you will not.")*

Determination is very powerful; it transcends the gloom of discouragement! It can make you go beyond your natural limits and do what you never thought you could. Rudy Ruettiger, was one of those very determined people. Ever since he was a small child he had always had a burning desire to play on the Notre Dame football team. His determination helped him to conquer his trials and barriers and eventually lead him to succeed in joining the team.

Rudy's story shows that if you are determined to fulfill your dreams you will. Rudy was determined to get into Holy Cross College, then into Notre Dame, and then on the Notre Dame football team and in a game. All of this proves that determination and belief in the person that you were designed by God to be will not only help you to succeed in accomplishing your desired life goals, but also overcome discouragement as well! Rudy's determination and faith got him in a game, and into a play that ended up sacking the quarterback. He fulfilled his destiny and so can YOU![5]

## THIRD: UNDERSTANDING REMOVES OBSTACLES

(*"...and doubtless he would grant you an interview, and point out the readiest way to remove, or overcome, the obstacles which have thwarted you."*)

Discouragement and obstacles seem to go hand in hand! Former congressmen Frank A. Clark said, *"If you can find a path with no obstacles, it probably doesn't lead anywhere."*[6] I believe obstacles are placed in our path for a reason. Without them, you would never know the depths of the type of person that you really are. Adversity has the effect of bringing to the surface your talents and gifts, which otherwise would have lain dormant and unexposed. Consequently, the biggest challenges aren't the obstacles themselves, but rather the challenge lies in learning from them and understanding them so as not to keep revisiting the same adversities throughout your life.

## Getting to know your obstacles

Obstacles can block your path, derail your efforts, and demand that you stop and think through your next steps carefully. If you are facing obstacles in your life and are stumped about how to get around or over them, learning a few basic facts about what is holding you back might help.

So here are a few facts about understanding your obstacles that may help you on your journey with facing adversity.

**1 - Obstacles, by their very nature, challenge you to grow, change and adapt.** Whether they arise from your personal past or are just part of the path you have chosen, they have the habit of getting you out of habits, teaching you about the way the world works, and making you grow stronger and more flexible. We all hope our life will be a "cake walk," but in reality, your obstacles make you work for what you want and hopefully keep you emotionally and physically healthy in the process, in particular if you choose to want to understand them better. Life can be either a merry-go-round or a roller coaster when it comes to the obstacles you face. Try to start looking at them as opportunities rather than adversities.

**2 - The secret of how to overcome your obstacles is learning how to turn them to your advantage.** Many things stop or delay you on your journey through life. Yet behind every hurdle is a reason for its existence. Sometimes high walls keep you out of dangerous places. Sometimes they are just opportunities to learn what a ladder is for. To turn obstacles to your advantage, you need to see the reason behind the obstacle as well as the opportunity it brings you. That opportunity can be to learn something new, develop a sharper skill, or find a better path. To allow your obstacle to intimidate you where you do nothing, or the same old same old, is to just keep sitting on the track as the train barrels toward you!

**3 - Obstacles naturally arise to keep you in balance as you open up to change.** Just start to think seriously about making some changes in your life and suddenly obstacles can appear overnight. Often obstacles make you slow down or stop so past unresolved issues, obsolete perspectives, and outdated ideas can take center stage to be resolved. Often fighting your way through the obstacles actually tests your resolve and prepares you for the new reality you want to create in your life. There's an old saying that says, "be careful what you wish for." Obstacles actually build in a level of safeguard by acting as a natural form of resistance that keeps your life in balance. Without that balance, you would hurtle at light speed into the things you want but that are not necessarily the best for you. By having to slow down to get around the road blocks and speed bumps of life, you have time to make sure you wholeheartedly want to arrive where you are headed.

**4 – The very things that slow you down can also act as helping you choose the right path.** Sometimes obstacles make you change course or rethink your approach to a person, issue, or next step. They can often work as guides pointing you, if you listen, in the direction of a better path. Sometimes, they are just like a porter on a train, checking you to make sure you have the right ticket and are catching the right train. In hindsight, some obstacles did you a favor by making you take another path through life. Sometimes going around in circles is the right way because that is the only path that leads you out of a maze.

## Success over discouragement

Succeeding in your life goals involves learning and then successfully applying a number of self-determination skills, such as goal-setting, understanding your abilities and disabilities, problem-solving, and learning how to deal with setbacks and discouragement. The personal process of learning, using, and self-evaluating these skills in a variety of settings is at the heart of winning over times of discouragement in your life.

People define success in many different ways. For instance, a few people who have had to battle discouragement with disabilities have said the following:

1.  *"Success is defined by who you are, what you believe in, and what you think it means to be successful. For some it is money; for others it could be relationships, family, jobs, religion, or education. I believe that success is reaching my own personal dreams. I'm not done with my dreams, but know that I have been successful so far because I've worked toward my goals*

*regardless of my discouragements and disability.*" (a college student who is deaf)

2.  "*Success is possessing the capability for self-determination through times of discouragement. Self-determination is the ability to decide what I want to do with my life, and then to act on that decision.*" (a high school student who is blind)

3.  "*A successful life is one where I can be actively engaged in creative activities that make a contribution to the lives of others. Success is a kind of by-product and NOT an end in itself!*" (a professor who is blind)

4.  "*To me, having a successful life is being able to do things independently for myself, and not always have someone there to do things for me. It's achieving my goals through the daily challenges that I face on my own terms and at my own speed.*" (a high school student with a mobility and orthopedic impairment)[7]

I am not suggesting that you are to be "psychosomatic" (mind over matter) when it comes to you and discouragement. Without question, discouragement is very real and has been known to disable the most confident people in history! That being said, discouragement, if not properly and effectively

160

addressed in your life, will reach out its tentacles like an angry squid and slowly squeeze out every bit of hope that is in you!

Discouragement is designed to be crippling and debilitating, it's a future destroyer, it attacks your hopes, dreams, enthusiasm, faith, and aspirations for life! But there is another side of discouragement as well, a side that we hardly ever see or even want to acknowledge. That being the job of a teacher! In the 2005 blockbuster movie, Batman Begins, Alfred Pennyworth (Bruce Wayne's butler) says to Bruce Wayne who is distraught over losing his family's mansion to a fire, "*Why do we fall, sir? So that we might better learn to pick ourselves up.*"[8] Without the learned experiences of discouragement, you would never understand what was right and applicable from that which isn't. Discouragement teaches you that the direction you are preceding in must not be working, that there is yet a better way! Discouragement teaches you to pick yourself up when things seem to be working against you. Consequently, if discouragement never visited you, you would be just like the wind-up toy that keeps bouncing against the wall making no progress while all the time going nowhere and losing energy to boot!

The great English clergymen, Robert South (1634-1716) once said, "*Defeat should never be a source of discouragement but rather a fresh stimulus.*"[9] Discouragement no doubt has already crossed your life's path, if it hasn't, stay tuned, it will! But the next time it does, use it as a "fresh stimulus," a new springboard for re-evaluating the direction you have taken. Instead of seeing discouragement as a foe that has come to rob you of your desired goals or dreams in life, use it as a tool for good as you take time to re-chart your course in the direction of smoother and more pleasant waters.

## Chapter Eleven

# You and Your Future

*I know what I'm doing. I have it all planned out—plans*
*to take care of you, not abandon you, plans to give you*
*the future you hope for.* -Jeremiah 29:11 (The
Message)

God's plans are that you will succeed in your life journey,
not fail! And even though your past may have been difficult or
even emotionally painful, God still has a plan for you...He always
has! The "inconvenient interruptions" of life have a way of
clouding a person's view of a bright and prosperous future. It's
possible that you may even have mentally blocked out any hope
of achieving your goals, dreams, or aspirations in life as a result of
the wounding, discouragement, and disappointment you've
carried throughout the years. Or perhaps your life has not seen
dramatic circumstances but still you have felt that the chances for
a bright and encouraging future are minimal at best. Life is very
real, and as a result, can be pretty uncooperative at times. Isaac
Asimov put it this way, "*Life is pleasant. Death is peaceful. It's the*
*transition that's troublesome.*"[1]

In the movie, "Man On Fire," a former CIA assassin and
presently an alcoholic decadent man John Creasy (Denzel

Washington), is hired by the industrialist Samuel Ramos to be the bodyguard of his young daughter Pita and his wife Lisa while in Mexico City. Pita buys John Creasy a necklace with a St. Jude medal on it. She said, "St. Jude is the patron saint of lost causes." Later that night while in his apartment, Creasy, as was his habit every evening, reached for his fifth of Jack Daniels. As he did, he noticed his Bible on the end table. After a moment of reflection, Creasy screwed the top back on the fifth of whiskey and then reached for his Bible and began to read it.[2]

John Creasy's past was traumatized and, consequently, the guilt and self-condemnation he felt, caused him to conclude that any chance for a bright future was impossible. Now most likely your life circumstances aren't as dramatic as John Creasy's. But when a person entertains thoughts that lead them to believe that their future is perhaps a "lost cause," then it's time for an overhaul! Let's take a look at a healthy way of mapping out a path to an encouraging and promising future!

## Mapping your future

Wouldn't it be awesome to have a map of your life goals that would allow you to see exactly where you are, where you want to be, how to get there, and all the signs along the way to steer you in the right direction to your destination? Oh, and also a "firewall" that will block out any obstructions that try to throw you off your course for success! You may be thinking, "Right, Fred, things like that just don't happen so easy!" You're right, they don't happen so easy, but nonetheless they can happen! You really can plot out your life goals, dreams, hopes, and aspirations. Certainly not that "every one" of your longings will systematically come true without a degree of challenge or even failure at times, but your Creator really has provided for you a future, with plans to take care of you, not abandon you and give you hope! In this case, "seeing [isn't] believing"...it's the reverse, in order to see it, you must first believe it! In order to experience the great and blessed future that has been purposed for you, you must first lay hold of the divine fact that you have one! If you can't start there, then there is no way that you can effectively proceed, because your "coded messages" are kicking in, defining you as having little or no chance to succeed in life. Here is where you need to shift it into "De-code" gear so as to be able to "believe then receive!" This isn't some Jedi mind trick...your future really is bright if you will only believe in the greater YOU that has been designed by God to achieve amazing and life changing things!

If you dare to apply what I have been sharing with you in the previous chapters, you will be laying the groundwork for a solid foundation to start building your life future on! So, what would your future look like if you were to map it out? Let's take a look at three questions regarding your life goals.

## QUESTION 1: Where exactly <u>are you</u> on the road to your life goals?

In order to get where you want to go, you must first know where you are. Assessing your personal/emotional liabilities can have an enormous positive effect on the outcome of your future. I've shared with you throughout this book models, insights, and methods by which you can apply change in your life. By considering to implement these principles into the fiber of your life plan, is to not only set yourself up for a more successful future, but also to make you aware of the areas that are presently holding you back from achieving that success. What is your present view of you? What messages & signals have been defining you? Where do you fall on the temperament chart? How about your self talk, ownership level, and mind & soul care? Do you believe in the greater YOU? And are you free to dream dreams as well as light the darkness in your corner of the world? And how would you assess your discouragement level? To answer these questions is to more accurately pinpoint where you are on the road to your life plan and desired future. As the old saying goes, *"if you shoot at nothing, you'll hit it every time!"* It's time now to start aiming at the "bull's eye" that has been designated for your amazing and successful future! Clearly acknowledging and wanting to understand your personal liabilities is the first step in getting to where you want to go!

## QUESTION 2: Where exactly <u>do you want to be</u> on the road to your life goals?

Goal setting is a powerful process of thinking, praying, and pondering about your ideal future, as well as for motivating yourself to turn your vision of the future into reality.

The process of setting goals helps you choose where you want to go in life. By knowing what you want to achieve, you then know where you have to concentrate your efforts. You'll also quickly spot the distractions that would otherwise lure you from your course.

The first step in setting personal goals is to consider what you want to achieve in your lifetime. Setting lifetime goals gives you the overall perspective that shapes all other aspects of your decision making.

In looking at a broad, balanced coverage of the most important areas in your life, try to set goals in some of these categories (or in other categories that are important to you).

### *Artistic:*
Do you want to achieve any artistic goals? If so, what are they?

### *Temperament:*

Is any part of your temperament holding you back? Is there any part of the way that you behave, respond or react that upsets you or others? If so, set a goal to improve your behavior in the down sides of your temperament by finding solutions through ownership for the issues that you carry.

### *Career:*

What would you like to do, and what level would you want to reach in your career?

### *Education:*

Is there any knowledge you want to acquire in particular? What information, educational degree, and skills will you need to achieve your goals?

### *Family:*

Are you presently married or are you planning on being married? How would you better like to see your relationship mature? What negatives and positives do you bring into the relationship? If you have children, in what ways would you like to improve as a parent?

### *Financial:*

Are you in debt? In what ways can you be free of your debt as well as setting boundaries in your life that will stand as safeguards so as not to get back into debt? In what ways would you like to financially plan for your future? How will you get there?

### Physical:

Are there health goals you want to achieve? Do you want good health throughout your "golden years?" What steps are you going to take to achieve these goals for your future health?

### Faith:

Are you satisfied with where you are in your faith? Is there a great degree of peace and security in your relationship with God or do you find that you struggle here? In what ways can you strengthen your spiritual journey?

### Public Service:

In what ways would you like to reach out in helping your fellow man? If so, how would you like to accomplish these acts of compassion and kindness?

In setting your lifetime goals, you can catch a glimpse of the kind of future you are mapping out for yourself as well as charting your course in the direction you want to be in.

## QUESTION 3: How exactly <u>do you plan</u> to get there?

Doing personal assessment on yourself can be of great benefit in preparing you with your plans for the future. Addressing the areas in your life that have caused you "down time" in your quest for successfully pursuing your goals, can be immensely helpful in planning for a brighter and more emotionally secure future. Here is a quick "Assess Test."

- Are you prone to depression and/or anxiety? If so, have you begun to address this through your minister/pastor or a counseling therapist?
- Are you content in life or do you struggle with being content and satisfied?
- Are there areas in your life that are controlling you? Examples: alcohol, drugs, pornography, tobacco, food, spending, validation, etc. If so, what are you doing to address these "future robbers?"
- Are you doing some form of exercise on a weekly basis? If not, are you willing to start?
- Do you get the proper amount of sleep each night (8 hours) or do you struggle with sleeping?
- Do you eat a good, healthy diet or do you eat what you can when you can?
- Do you have anyone to talk to about the things in your life that upset you or stress you out?
- Do you feel good about what you do? (This applies to the work of your life, whether it is at a job, at home caring for children, as a full-time student, etc.)

- What is your opinion of YOU?  Do you have a healthy self-image or a poor one?  What are you doing to feel better about YOU?
- Is there a secure connection with God in your life (or) do you find that you have many questions regarding your faith?

By addressing the above questions, you are planning as well as constructing your way toward an emotionally, relationally, physically, occupationally, and spiritually healthy future!  To not consider these questions is to continue to place a band-aid over a potential cancer in your life's journey that will snuff out the flame that God has intended to shine vibrantly bright!  Michelangelo wisely said, "*The greatest danger for most of us is not that our aim is too high and we miss it, but that it is too low and we reach it.*"[3]  If you are not planning your future through assessing the areas that will hinder you from getting there, then you are lowing your aim and, consequently, missing "...*the goal for the prize of the upward call of God...*" in your life! (Philippians 3:14)

There is an African Proverb that says, "*For tomorrow belongs to the people who prepare for it today.*"[4]  If you desire a promising, fulfilling, secure, faith-filled, and meaningful future, then start planning and building it into your life's fiber today!

Stubbornly refuse to allow negative past experiences to come between you and your destiny. Sir Winston Churchill said: "*If we open a quarrel between the past and the present, we shall find that we have lost the future.*"[5]

Who better to believe in your future than YOU? Remember, you are the one person that you will never get away from! So what do you say? Maybe now is the time to start taking the steps to discover that greater YOU. Just think, if you really want to, you can now begin to start building the foundation for your life that will lead to an incredible, amazing and liberating journey that will move you in the direction of finally being FREE TO BE YOU!

# Notes

## Chapter 1: A Different View of You

1. Roosevelt, Franklin D., "The Quotation Page-Quotation #3250 from Laura Moncur's Motivational Quotations"; available from http://www.brainyquotes.com/quote/3250.html; Internet; accessed 12 June 2007.

2. Roosevelt, Franklin D., "The Quotation Page-Quotation #37962 from Laura Moncur's Motivational Quotations"; available from http://www.quotationspage.com/quote/37962.html; Internet; accessed 12 June 2007.

3. Maltz, Maxwell, "Brainy Quotes"; available from http://www.brainyquotes.com/quotes/quotes/m/maxwellmall57457.html; Internet; accessed 13 June 2007.

4. Franklin, Benjamin, "Quote DB"; available at http://www.quotedb.com/quotes/3827; Internet; accessed 12 June 2007.

5. Pogo, "I Go Pogo"; available from http://www.igopogo.com/we_have_met.html; Internet; accessed 12 June 2007.

## Chapter 2: You and Your Identity

1. May, Rollo, "Brainy Quote"; available from http://www.brainyquote.com/quotes/authors/r/rollo_may.html; Internet; accessed 13 June 2007.

2. Lincoln, Abraham, "Annual Message to Congress - Concluding Remarks"; available from http://showcase.netins.net/web/creative/lincoln/speeches/congress.htm; Internet; accessed 17 June 2008.

3. Lincoln, Abraham, "Quotes & Poems"; available from http://quotesandpoems.com/quotes/showquotes/subject/american-presidential-quotes/5512; Internet; accessed 13 June 2007.

173

4. Stallone, Sylvester. 1982. Rocky 3.

5. Arendt, Hannah, "Hannah Arendt"; available from
http://www.quoteworld.org/quotes/536; Internet; accessed 17 June 2008.

6. Boese, Paul, "Paul Boese Quotes"; available from
http://www.thinkexist.com/quotation/forgiveness_does_not_change_the_past_it
_does/9267.html; Internet; accessed 13 June 2007.

7. Assagioli, Roberto, "Roberto Assagioli Quotes"; available from
http://www.thinkexist.com/quotation/without_forgiveness_life_is_goverened_by
_an/177996.html; Internet; accessed 13 June 2007.

8. Newton, Sir Isaac, "Sir Isaac Newton Quotes"; available from
http://www.thinkexist.com/quotation/if_i_have_seen_farther_than_others_it_is
_because/11096.html; Internet; accessed 13 June 2007.

9. King, Jr. Dr. Martin Luther, "Dr. Martin Luther King Quotes"; available
from
http://www.thinkexist.com/quotation/we_must_accept_finite_disappointment-
but_never/8113.html; Internet; accessed 13 June 2007.

10. Mother Teresa, "Mother Teresa Quotes"; available from
http://www.thinkexist.com/quotation/the_hunger_for_love_is_much_more_diff
icult_to/8148.html; Internet; accessed 13 June 2007.

11. Emerson, Ralph Waldo, "Raplh Waldo Emerson Quotes"; available from
http://www.thinkexist.com/quotation/our_strength_grows_out_of_our/191915.
html; Internet; accessed 13 June 2007.

12. Aesop's Fable, "Ancient/Classical History"; available from
http://www.ancienthistory.about.com/library/bl/bl_aesop_dog_oyster.html;
Internet; accessed 13 June 2007.

13. Lincoln, Abraham, "The Everyday Life of Abraham Lincoln"; available
from
http://www.Infomotions.com/etexts/Gutenberg/dirs/1/4/0/0/14004/14004.html;
Internet; accessed 14 June 2007.

14. Hewett, James S., Illustrations Unlimited. (Wheaton: Tyndale House
Publishers, 1988), 159.

15. Graham, Martha, "The Pachmama Alliance"; available from http://www.awakening thedreamer.org/content/view/39/60/; Internet; accessed 14 June 2007.

16. Hesse, Herman, "The Story of Emil Sinclair's Youth"; available from http://www.sikhspectrum.com/022003/demain.html; Internet; accessed 15 June 2007.

17. Hybels, Bill, "Bill Hybels Quotes"; available from http://www.en.thinkexist.com/quotation/god_wants_to_father_all_of_us_until_ we-re_dead/330987.html; Internet; accessed 15 June 2007.

18. St. Augustine, "Lord Jesus Let me Know Myself"; available from http://www.preces-latinae.org/thesarus/Filius/NoverimMe.html; Internet; accessed 15 June 2007.

# Chapter 3: Your Amazing Temperament

1. Arno, Dr.'s Richard & Phyllis (Pages 23-34), *Sarasota Academy of Christian Counseling*, ©All Rights Reserved.

2. Notes from class lecture.

# Chapter 4: You and Self-Talk

1. Jung, Dr. Carl Gustav, "Brainy Quote"; available from http://www.brainyquote.com/quotes/c/carljung101266.html; Internet; accessed 16 June 2007.

2. Saint Francis of Assisi, "Song of Praise"; available from http://www.americancatholic.org/Messenger/Oct1996/feature1.asp; Internet; accessed 22 June 2007.

3. Mother Teresa, "World Net Daily"; available from http://www.worldnetdaily.com/news/article.asp?ARTICLE_ID=59960; Internet; accessed 23 June 2007.

4. Lee, Bruce, "Bruce Lee Quotes"; available from http://www.thinkexist.com/quotation/all_fixed_set_patterns_are_incapable_of/2 62671.html; Internet; accessed 23 June 2007.

5. Hamilton, Bethany, "Most Inspiring Person of the Year Award"; available from http://www.beliefnet.com/story/137/story_13707_1.html; Internet; accessed 28 June 2007.

6. Lincoln, Abraham, "Selected Quotations by Abraham Lincoln"; available from http://showcase.netins.net/web/creative/lincoln/speeches/quotes.htm; Internet; accessed 18 June 2008.

# Chapter 5: You and the Power of Ownership

1. Gandhi, Mahatma, "PEACE Quote View"; available from http://www.schipul.com/en/q/?1463; Internet; accessed 17 June 2008.

2. Smiles, Samuel, "Quotes to Inspire You"; available from http://www.cybernation.com/victory/quotations/subjects/quotes_achievement.ht ml; Internet; accessed 14 July 2007.

3. Ruiz, Don Miguel, "Four Agreements Necessary for Wisdom"; available from http//www.katinkahesslink.net/other/first-agreement.html; Internet; accessed 12 August 2007.

4. Davis, Miles, "USA Today", available from http://www.usatoday.com/money/smallbusiness/columnist/edmunds/2004-12-08-davis_x.html; Internet; accessed 25 August 2007.

5. Joyce, James, "Brainy Quote"; available from http://www.brainyquotes.com/quotes/authors/j/james_joyce.html; Internet; accessed 4 September 2007.

6. Kennedy, John F., "Brainy Quote"; available from http://www.brainyquote.com/quotes/authors/j/john_f_kennedy.html; Internet; accessed 20 September 2007.

7. Roosevelt, Franklin D., "Brainy Quote"; available from http://www.brainyquote.com/quotes/authorsf/franklin_d_roosevelt.html; Internet; accessed 21 September 2007.

8. Southmayd, Alex, "Give It Forward Today"; available from http://www.giveitforwardtoday.ord/index.php?page=bio; Internet; accessed 28 September 2007.

9. Spurgeon, Charles H., "Quote Garden"; available from http://www.quotegarden.com/ssweetest-day.html; Internet; accessed 4 October 2007.

10. "Act of Humility"; available from http://www.latinmasses.ca/act-humility.html; Internet; accessed 8 October 2007.

11. McLuhan, Marshall, "Marshall McLuhan Quotes"; available from http://www.thinkexist.com/quotation-we_drive_into_the_future_using_only_our_rear_view/152904.html; Internet; accessed 16 October 2007.

# Chapter 6: Nourishing Your Mind and Soul

1. *The American Heritage Dictionary of the English Language: Fourth Edition.* (Wilmington, MA: Houghton Mifflin, 2000).

2. Brown, John Seely, "Quotes by John Seely Brown"; available from http://www.absolutleyhonest.com/authors/John20%Seely%20Brown_quotes.html; Internet; accessed 20 October 2007

3. Plato, "Plato Quotes"; available from http://www.thinkexist,com/quotation/good_actions_give_strength_to_ourselves_and/8216.html; Internet; accessed 28 August 2007.

4. Definition of the word "filter", "The Free Dictionary"; available from http://www.thefreedictionary.com/compensating+filter; Internet; accessed 22 October 2007.

5. Rausch, Bob, *I Don't Dress Dead People.* (Norcross, GA: 1 Executive Energy, 2007), 125.

# Chapter 7: Discovering the Greater You

1. Drucker, Peter, "Gallup Management Journal"; available from http://gmj.gallup.com/content/1147/Now-Discover-Your-Strengths-Book-Center.aspx; Internet; accessed 26 October 2007.

2. Buckingham, Marcus & Donald Clifton, "Now Discover Your Strengths"; available from http://www.buildyourfreedom.com/tl/tl03h.html; Internet; accessed 30 October 2007.

3. Clifton, Donald, "Your Natural Talents Gifts and Strengths"; available from http://www.wheatoncollege.edu/Filene/Toolkit/selfExplore/talents.html; Internet; accessed 18 June 2008.

4. Aristotle, "Career Change Pathways"; available from http://www.careerchangepathways.com/com; Internet; accessed 30 January 2007.

5. Moss-Kanter, Rosa Beth, "Brainy Quote"; available from http://www.brainyquote.com/quotes/authors/r/rosabeth_moss_kanter.html; Internet; accessed 12 November 2007.

6. Leider, Richard, "Searching for Direction: #3 Explore Career Possibilities"; available from http://www.careerclues.org/explore-career-possibilities.html; Internet; accessed 17 June 2008.

7. Friedman, Bonnie, "Understanding Yourself"; available from http://www.wheatoncollege.edu/Filene/Toolkit/selfExplore; Internet; accessed 20 December 2007.

8. Wiz, Dr., "Washington Roebling Story"; available from http://bethei.blogspot.com/2007/07/determination.html; Internet; accessed 14 January 2008.

9. Kansas, "Dust in the Wind"; available from http://www.lyrics007.com/Kansas%20Lyrics/Dust%20In%20The%20Wind%20%20%20Correct%20Lyrics.html; Internet; accessed 18 June 2008.

## Chapter 8: You and Your Dreaming Dreams

1. Carroll, Lewis, "Alice's Adventures in Wonderland"; available from http://www.quoteworld.org/quotes/2453; Internet; accessed 17 January 2008.

2. Cheever, Susan, "Brian Wilson's Story"; available from http://www.time.com/time/time100/heros/profile/wilson01.html; Internet; accessed 23 January 2008.

3. Kushner, Rabbi Harold, "Overcoming Life's Disappointments"; available from http://www.leighbureau.com/speaker.asp?id=102; Internet; accessed 12 February 2008.

4. Hughes, Langston, "A Dream Deferred"; available from
http://www.cswnet.com/~menamc/langston.htm; Internet; accessed 18 June
2008.

5. "Fred Smith Story"; available from
http://www.acheivement.org/autodoc/page/smi0pro-1; Internet; accessed 18
February 2008.

6. Twain, Mark, "Twain Quotes"; available from
http://www.twainquotes.com/optimist.html; Internet; accessed 29 February
2008.

7. Aerosmith, "Lyrics Freak"; available from
http://www.lyricsfreak.com/a/aerosmith/dream+on_20004389.html; Internet;
accessed 19 February 2008.

# Chapter 9: You and Lighting the Darkness

1. Tiedje, Kristen, "Lighting the Darkness"; available from
http://findarticles.com/p/articles/mi_m0KZH/is_/ai_30150321; Internet;
accessed 22 February 2008.

2. Blevins, Lea, "Couple Devotes Life to Others"; available from
http://findarticles.com/p/articles/mi_qn4176/is_20071108/ai_n21105679;
Internet; accessed 28 February 2008.

3. History of the Salvation Army, "Becoming the Hands of God"; available
from http://www.salvationarmy.org/ihq%5Cwww_sa.nsf/vw-
sublinks/5622F771BD70A75A80256D4E003AE0A3?opendocument;
Internet; accessed 2 March 2008.

4. Wurst, Nancy Henderson, "Doing the Right Thing"; available from
http://www.nads.org/pages_new/human_interest/doingtherightthing.html;
Internet; accessed 8 March 2008.

5. Mastony, Colleen, "Doctors Without Borders"; available from
http://www.chicagotribune.com/news/nationworld/chi-070512guineaworm-
story,0,0878862.story; Internet; accessed 17 March 2008.

6. Schweitzer, Albert. "Kiva Friends"; available from
http://www.kivafriends.com/index.php?topic=458.msg31453;topicseen;
Internet; accessed 20 March 2008.

7. St. Francis of Assisi, "World Prayers"; available from
http://www.worldprayers.orgframeit.cgi?/archive/prayers/invocations/lord_make
_me_an_instrument.html; Internet; accessed 14 April 2008.

## Chapter 10: You and Discouragement

1. "Discouragement"; available from
http://wordnet.princeton.edu/perl/webwn?s=discouragement; Internet;
accessed 17 June 2008.

2. Warren, Rick, "Some Cures for Discouragement"; available from
http://www.cbn.com/spirituallife/BibleStudyAndTheology/Discipleship/Warre
n_Discouragement.aspx; Internet; accessed 28 March 2008.

3. Lincoln, Abraham, "Letter to George Latham"; available from
http://showcasenetins.net/web/creative/lincoln/speeches/latham.html; Internet;
accessed 18 March 2008.

4. Plasse, Sean, "Overcoming Dyslexia and Turning a Corner in Life";
available from http://www.npr.org/templates/story/story.php?storyId=6425164;
Internet; accessed 18 March 2008.

5. Wikipedia, "Rudy Ruettiger"; available from
http://en/wikipedia.org/wiki/Daniel_Ruettiger; Internet; accessed 3 March
2008.

6. Clark, Frank A., "Frank A. Clark Quotes"; available from
http://www.thinkexist.com/quotation/if_you_can_find_a_pathwith_no_obstacle
s-it/205851.html; Internet; accessed 24 March 2008.

7. Burgstahler, Sheryl Dr., "Taking Charge: Stories of Success and Self-
Determination"; Quotes 1-4; available from
http://www.washington.edu/doit/Brochures/Technology/charge.html; Internet;
accessed 26 March 2008.

8. "Quote from Batman Begins"; available from
http://www.imbd.com/title/tt0372784/quotes;Internet; accessed 8 April 2008.

9. South, Robert (1634-1716), "Brainy Quote"; available from
http://www.brainyquote.com/quotes/quotes/b/bishoprobe155168.html.

# Chapter 11: You and Your Future

1. Asimov, Isaac, "The Resistance"; available from http://theresistance.tumblr.com/post/35757874/life-is-pleasant-death-is-peaceful-its-the; Internet; accessed 12 April 2008.

2. Washington, Denzel. 2004. Man on Fire, 20th Century Fox.

3. Michelangelo, "Innovation & creativity Quotes"; available from http://www.innovationtools.com/quotes/quotes.asp; Internet; accessed 14 May 2008.

4. "African Proverb Quotes"; available from http://www.think exist.com/quotation/for_tomorrow_belongs_to_the_people_who_prepare/174 510.html; Internet; accessed 16 May 2008.

5. Churchill, Sir Winston, "Quotes, Sayings and Proverbs About the Future"; available from http://www.specialty-calendars.com/future.html; Internet; accessed 20 May 2008.

Printed in the United States
203322BV00003B/1-156/P

9 780979 805332